THE WIT OF CRICKET

THE WIT
OF CRICKET

SECOND INNINGS

Compiled and Updated by
Barry Johnston

Illustrations by John Ireland

HODDER &
STOUGHTON

First published in Great Britain in 2022 by Hodder & Stoughton
An Hachette UK company

1

A CIP catalogue record for this title is available from the British Library

Hardback ISBN 9781399703673
Trade Paperback ISBN 9781399703710
eBook ISBN 9781399703703

Typeset in Sabon MT by Hewer Text UK Ltd, Edinburgh
Printed and bound in Great Britain by Clays Ltd, Elcograf S.p.A.

Hodder & Stoughton policy is to use papers that are natural, renewable
and recyclable products and made from wood grown in sustainable
forests. The logging and manufacturing processes are expected to
conform to the environmental regulations of the country of origin.

Hodder & Stoughton Ltd
Carmelite House
50 Victoria Embankment
London EC4Y 0DZ

www.hodder.co.uk

To Aggers, Bearders, Blowers,
CMJ, Dickie, Sir Frederick,
Johnners and Richie

CONTENTS

FOREWORD

Over the last twenty years the world of cricket has been transformed, almost beyond recognition. Twenty20 cricket was first played in England in 2003, quickly followed by the Indian Premier League, the Big Bash in Australia, and even the Afghan Premier League, introducing the game to millions of new fans around the world. Legendary players have retired and new superstars have emerged.

As the money earned by the top cricketers and their teams has risen, so too has their professionalism, and as Jimmy Anderson points out in this book, pranks have slightly become a thing of the past. But there are still plenty of laughs to be had on and off the field. In particular, I would like to know the identity of the phantom sock snipper in the England dressing-room during the 2015 Ashes series!

I grew up listening to my father, the BBC cricket commentator Brian Johnston, telling jokes and stories. He remembered funny anecdotes in the same way that other people collect stamps and he loved retelling them in his after-dinner speeches and in his one-man show *An*

Evening with Johnners. Most of those stories were about cricket – it is a game that has inspired more humour than any other sport – and they continue to make us laugh.

In this updated and expanded edition of *The Wit of Cricket*, I have kept the best of the original stories and anecdotes from past and present Test and county players, as well as the most famous cricketing sledges, the gaffes and giggles in the *Test Match Special* commentary box, and humorous extracts from the modern cricket classics *Penguins Stopped Play*, *Batting on the Bosphorus*, *Rain Men* and *Fatty Batter*.

However, it is thirteen years since the first edition of this book was published in 2009, and some of these stories were originally written back in the 1970s and 1980s. So I have removed a number of the older anecdotes that are not as funny with the passage of time.

Names have changed too: Calcutta is now Kolkata, Madras is Chennai, and so on. More recently, batsmen are now called batters – like bowlers and fielders – and it seems so obvious that one wonders why it has taken so long. One can't rewrite history, though, so all the original stories in this edition still refer to Calcutta and batsmen, and only the newest stories reflect the current name changes.

I have added five new chapters, including more cricketing tales from India, Australia and the West Indies, and dozens of new anecdotes from players such as Alastair

Cook, Joe Root, Ben Stokes, Matthew Hayden, Justin Langer and Sachin Tendulkar. There are also more funny stories from the commentary box by Jonathan Agnew, Peter Baxter, Daniel Norcross and the late Christopher Martin-Jenkins, and some witty extracts from the excellent books *Fibber in the Heat* and *Unlimited Overs*.

Whether you prefer T20, the Hundred, ODIs or Test matches (or, hopefully, enjoy all four), cricket is still the funniest game of them all!

Barry Johnston
2022

A FUNNY GAME

Christopher Martin-Jenkins:

I love spring – it is the season of showers and callow hopefulness, with apologies to Keats. As opposed to autumn, which I think it was Denis Norden once observed, is the time when a really true cricket lover woke up one morning to find out that his wife had left him in April!

Jimmy Anderson:

How can something that lasts five days end in a draw, when T20 gives you a result in a few hours?

It's mostly Americans who ask that question. Try to look at it this way.

Cricket is *Revolver* by the Beatles. T20 is 'Yellow Submarine'. Test cricket is 'Tomorrow Never Knows'.

They both belong on the same album. 'Yellow Submarine' is great. It's catchy and instantly recognisable. Everyone knows 'Yellow Submarine'. It doesn't matter what age you are, you get it. However, if you listen to it ten times in a row, you'll be so saccharined up to the eyeballs, that you'll be cross-eyed. You would be forgiven for wondering, 'There must be more to the Beatles than this.'

T20 is the same. It has action, it has fireworks, it's over quickly. You watch it and think, 'Oh, I get it.' It is, if you will, a gateway drug.

'Tomorrow Never Knows' is tricky at first, irregular and at odds with the other song structures on *Revolver*. It has rules and laws all of its own. Its genius is that as you live with it, you keep finding new things. There are layers on it that make it last forever. Its innovation is built into its DNA. Whatever has happened since in music, it still feels brand new. It's Test cricket. It survives. The band is the same. The instruments are the same. The album is the same. The music is very different.

Still with me?

Test cricket is a roast. T20 is an ice cream.

Ice cream is great. You eat it quickly. It's a rush. An ice cream is an ice cream. Nobody dislikes ice cream. But if you try to eat a diet solely of ice cream, you are going to become aware of its limitations very quickly.

A roast has *dimensions*. It gives you all the nourishment you need. You eat it slowly, appreciating the effort that has gone into making it. You look forward to roasts for a whole week. It has enough in it for everyone to find their own joy in there. Sometimes, a roast won't get it right. There's no gravy. The Yorkshires are missing. The potatoes are burned. It makes you wonder why you bother with roasts and why you wasted your time dreaming of it all week. When you get the right one, though, there's nothing better in the whole world.

I hope that helps!

Barry Johnston:

During the Third Test against South Africa at Lord's in August 2012, Jonathan Agnew was suddenly informed by the *Test Match Special* producer, Adam Mountford, that he would be interviewing the American rock star Alice Cooper in the tea interval. It turned out that Cooper was a great fan of cricket and he was at the match.

Shortly afterwards, Aggers was commentating with Geoffrey Boycott when the door to the box opened and in walked a man in his fifties with black hair down to his shoulders, wearing a black leather jacket and leather trousers, the rock legend himself, with his wife Sheryl. They sat down quietly at the back of the box.

Aggers turned to Boycott and said, 'Geoffrey, you will never guess who I am interviewing at tea.' He pointed behind him to the couple sitting in the corner and said proudly, 'Alice Cooper.'

It was clear from the blank expression on Boycott's face that he had never heard of the 'The Godfather of

Shock Rock'. As the players left the field for tea, he got up from his chair and went over to introduce himself.

'Hello, Alice, nice to meet you, luv,' he said – and shook hands with Mrs Cooper!

Henry Blofeld:

You never quite knew what was coming next with Brian Johnston. He was dynamite in the commentary box. There was a lovely moment at Headingley in 1976, when they were rather against intruders, because the year before, the George Davis fan club had dug up the pitch. George Davis was a London minicab driver who had been wrongly convicted of armed robbery and he was eventually freed. Funnily enough, when they rearrested him two years later, the High Court judge who sent him to prison was none other than my brother!

But anyway, they were dead against intruders at Headingley the following year and everything went swimmingly until just after lunch on Saturday when, from the position of the old, old pavilion, the one that Lord Hawke used to walk out from – there are two old pavilions at Headingley now – a little black-and-white dachshund cantered out into the middle. It was deter- mined to go to the Kirkstall Lane End, for some reason, and Brian was on the air.

He said, 'Well, we've got an intruder. A little black-and-white dachshund. He's a chirpy little chap. He's making a beeline for the Kirkstall Lane End. He's wrong-footed cover point, he's sold gully a dummy and, goodness me, he's now in the middle of the pitch. He's scratching away with his right front paw. Do you know, I think he's going to spend a penny. So too does umpire Tom Spencer. He's got one of the bowler's sleeveless jerseys and he's shooing it away. It's quite a promising little bullfight. But I can tell you at home that this dachshund is a fast bowler – and the reason I know he's a fast bowler is because he's got four short legs and his balls swing both ways!'

Jonny Bairstow:

My dad, the Yorkshire and England wicketkeeper David Bairstow, walked in the spotlight, a natural performer in the glare of it, but he would have been equally at home with anonymity. He also regularly hobnobbed with celebrity and aristocracy, but hated anything pompous or stuffy. He became pally with the multimillionaire Sir Paul Getty, who took him back to the lounge of his London flat for a drink.

The flat was about the size of a South American country and full of Persian rugs and Old Master paintings. Getty rang his butler to get my dad a drink. The butler had to walk about a hundred yards to reach them, the sound of his well-shined shoes eventually audible across a long corridor. He came into the room to open a cabinet that was within arm's reach of my dad's chair.

'Blimey,' my dad said. 'I could have saved you the trouble and poured my own!'

Barry Johnston:

Sir Tim Rice has been passionate about music and cricket all his life. He founded the Heartaches Cricket Club in 1973 and was President of MCC in 2002. In 1986 he even wrote a short musical with Andrew Lloyd Webber called *Cricket (Hearts and Wickets)* for Her Majesty Queen Elizabeth's sixtieth birthday celebrations at Windsor Castle.

In the early 1990s, Sir Tim was a team captain on the popular Radio 4 quiz show *Trivia Test Match*, loosely based on the rules of cricket. 'When I was invited to be a team captain,' he said later, 'and was told it would be with Willie Rushton and Brian Johnston, I said yes right away. It was my dream programme.'

By then he was a major figure in Hollywood and had won an Oscar for his song 'Whole New World' in the Walt Disney film *Aladdin*. He had tremendous difficulty trying to explain to the film executives at Disney why he had to take time off from working on their multi-million-dollar production of *The Lion King* to appear on a radio quiz show for £63 at a small cricket club in Surrey. Nevertheless, he returned to

England to be on the programme. 'Only Tim would fly back from Hollywood to appear on *Trivia Test Match*,' chuckled his regular team member Barry Cryer.

At the 67th Academy Awards in 1995, Sir Tim Rice and Elton John won the Oscar for Best Original Song for 'Can You Feel the Love Tonight' from *The Lion King*. In his acceptance speech, Sir Tim told the audience at the Shrine Auditorium, 'Many thanks to everyone at Disney, and in particular, as this is a musical award, Mr Hans Zimmer. I'd also like to thank Denis Compton, a boyhood hero of mine.'

This caused a certain amount of consternation back-stage. Finally, a flustered spokesman for the Academy of Motion Picture Arts and Sciences emerged to tell the assembled journalists, 'We don't know who Denis Compton is. He doesn't appear to be at Disney Studios or to have anything to do with *The Lion King*!'

Roger Morgan-Grenville:

The *Desiderata* of social cricket captaincy:

- Go placidly amid the noise and haste. *You are not in charge; you are merely responsible. There is a big difference.*
- Exercise caution in your business affairs, for the world is full of trickery. *The unseen but enthusiastically foreshadowed ringer that you are relying*

on for six probing overs and forty runs will be utterly useless. Always.

- Listen to others, even the dull and ignorant; they too have their story. *The fat bloke who volunteered at the party last night, and who is merely making up the numbers without any real involvement, once took five South African wickets for Namibia. If you don't try, you will never know.*

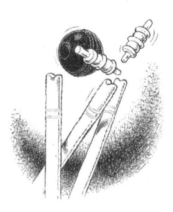

- Enjoy your achievements as well as your plans. *However, unlike the rest of your life, where you only regret what you didn't try, in cricket, you will normally regret just about everything you did try.*
- Take kindly the counsel of the years. *The minute you move second slip out, a soft, slow and insultingly easy catch will present itself to where he has just been standing. Normally next ball.*
- Nurture strength of spirit to shield you from sudden misfortune. *No. No one else on either side thought*

to put the urn on for tea forty minutes ago. That
was your job, whatever else happened to be on your
to-do list, and they will all stare at you when they
drink cold tea. And they would like you to magically produce drinks halfway through the innings,
too, even if you are the fielding captain.

- Remember what peace there may be in silence. *That
person who you stuck at number eleven because he
said, 'Don't worry, Skip. Put me where you like. I
don't mind where I go,' does mind. And he will hold
a grudge, as will his wife. She will bring it up three
years hence, when you meet again in a garden centre.*

- Beyond a wholesome discipline, be gentle on yourself. *But remember, you haven't actually won until
the metaphorical fat lady has sung, left the building, and done her entire weekly shop at Aldi.*

- You are a child of the universe. No less than the
trees and stars, you have a right to be here. *However,
don't kid yourself. Your job is simply to provide
twenty-two people with a lovely afternoon's cricket,
and your reward is to be allowed to be one of them.
Unless you have miscounted, and recruited one too
many, in which case you will be expected to stand
down and umpire both innings.*

- Be cheerful. Strive to be happy. *And, at the end of the
day, remember that you are simply the nipple of the
grease gun that allows the cogs of the season to rotate,*

and your ideas of Napoleonic grandeur are illusory.
You are the servant of the team, and not its master.

Dickie Bird:

There can hardly have been a more endearing character at Essex than Brian 'Tonker' Taylor. They called him that because he loved to give the ball an almighty tonk. He was both captain and wicketkeeper, and under him Essex were never short of ideas for getting batsmen out. Like one time, when Tonker set out to trick a compulsive hooker into playing the shot that would most likely prove his undoing.

Sure enough, the batsman, unable to resist the temptation, hooked the ball high and hard and was brilliantly caught just inside the ropes. Tonker and his team were ecstatic – until they realised that the umpire had called 'no-ball'.

All eyes turned accusingly towards the bowler and his frustrated colleagues tore him off a right strip, until the umpire explained that he had not called the bowler for over-stepping. He turned to Tonker. 'It was your fault, skipper,' he said to him. 'You've three men behind square leg.' The laws allowed for only two.

Tonker looked round in disbelief. He counted once. He counted twice. And he counted again. Then the penny dropped. 'Don't tell me you were counting that chap right on the boundary edge,' he muttered menacingly.

'Of course,' replied the umpire.

Tonker exploded, 'That's not a fielder, you fool, that's the bloody ice-cream man!'

Barry Johnston:

By the end of the 1990/91 Ashes series in Australia, Phil Tufnell had become a cult figure among the Australian supporters – but for all the wrong reasons. The Middlesex spinner made his Test debut in the Second Ashes Test at Melbourne on Boxing Day, but it was an inauspicious start to his Test career. England lost by eight wickets and Tufnell failed to take a wicket or score a run in either innings.

Things got even worse a few days later in a World Series day/night match at the Sydney Cricket Ground. The Australian Waugh brothers, Steve and Mark, were batting when they mixed up the call for a run and both ended up at the striker's end. Eddie Hemmings lobbed the ball gently to Phil Tufnell standing at the bowler's end, for what looked like an easy run-out, and Steve Waugh started to walk off. But not only did a nervous Tufnell fumble and drop the ball, he then picked it up and hurled it so wildly that it missed the stumps by a mile.

Unable to believe his luck, Steve Waugh jogged safely back to his crease while the whole Sydney Cricket Ground erupted with laughter, especially when Tufnell's ineptitude was replayed over and again, in slow motion, on the giant screen.

As the series progressed, so Tufnell's fielding went from bad to worse, and he admits that he spent most of his time in the field praying that the ball would not come anywhere near him. But the Australian crowds loved him for it and a group of supporters even founded the Phil Tufnell Fielding Academy. Phil was on the receiving end of a torrent of friendly abuse, but his favourite was when someone in the crowd called out, 'Hey Tufnell, lend me your brain, I'm building an idiot!'

Miles Jupp:

In the summer of 1991, my father took my brother Ed and me on a camping holiday to Ireland. Much of our time away was spent travelling to what the guide books described as 'places of interest'. However, none of them, I am ashamed to say, meant a great deal to eleven-year-old me. Being away from home didn't represent a wonderful opportunity to see new things and places. It simply meant that I was unable to watch the cricket on the television or check county scores on Teletext.

I mentioned this to my father in the car, though, and for my troubles I was rewarded with a wonderful discovery: BBC Radio 4's *Test Match Special*. This represented some sort of heaven to me: a radio show in which jolly men with jolly-sounding names and even jollier voices told listeners exactly what was happening in the cricket and filled in the gaps with chatter of more general interest, such as their best recent experiences involving cakes, or a discussion about whether or not hedgehogs should be given milk.

At one point during this game, and I had no idea what caused it, two of the men on this show collapsed into hysteria and for a minute and a half no sound emanated from the car's radio but that of their barely muffled shrieking and the occasional fragment of a croaked sentence.

Ed and I, sitting in the back of the car, found ourselves giggling too, whilst in the driver's seat my father let out a series of snorts and laughed so hard that he had to punch the horn four times in order to get a grip on himself!

Brian Johnston:

On the Mondays of a Test match at Lord's, the Queen always comes in the afternoon. It normally rains and there's hardly anybody there, but the teams are presented to her during the tea interval.

Robert Hudson was doing the commentary when the New Zealanders were being presented to the Queen and he said, 'It's a great occasion for these Commonwealth teams. It's a moment they will always forget!'

Who am I to talk? At the royal wedding of the Prince of Wales and Lady Diana, I was on Queen Anne's statue just in front of St Paul's Cathedral. She was called Brandy Annie, I was told, because she was a bit keen on the grog.

So I had a marvellous view standing there, because all the coaches and carriages drew up about six feet below me. I could see the Queen, with a rug over her knees, being helped out and so on.

I looked over my shoulder and said, 'I can see Lady Diana coming up Ludgate Hill, in her coach with her two escorts. The coach will come below me here, a page will open the door and she will be greeted by her father, Earl Spencer. Then they will walk up the steps together, into the pavilion . . . I mean, cathedral!'

Barry Johnston:

Before the 2013 Ashes series, David Gower created quite a stir in the media when he was asked if the 136-year rivalry between England and Australia was a clash of cultures.

He told the *Radio Times*, 'I'm tempted to say, how can you have a clash of cultures when you're playing against a country with no culture. That would almost be sledging.'

He went on to have a dig at the Aussie crowds, saying, 'The trouble is, if they've had ten cans of lager, their ability to come up with anything akin to Oscar Wilde diminishes. A lot of it therefore tends to be very stereotypical. It's the same with sledging on the field. There's a certain animal mentality. And if they sense a bit of weakness, they'll try it on more.'

Gower captained the victorious England team in the 1985 Ashes series and scored nine Test centuries against the old enemy. He revealed his secret.

'The great thing is just to smile, because the smile completely confuses them. But the best way to keep an Australian bowler quiet is simply to make runs. If you're 120 not out, they tend not to say much!'

Shane Warne, one of the biggest sledgers of them all, fired back, 'What's this about us having no f***ing culture?'

Gower replied, 'I rest my case.'

Jimmy Anderson:

The problem with being an international cricketer, on tour or otherwise, is the extremity of reaction to you, especially in India. It's very hard to gauge. In some places you are chased everywhere, followed around, carted about under high security. Then you'll be in a different part of the world a week later and it'll be, 'Jimmy Anderson? Never heard of you, mate.'

I came back from an India tour one year acclimatised to being on full alert at all times. Me and Graeme Swan had gone shopping in a department store.

Suddenly, from across the floor, I heard a manic and over-excited screech. 'JIIMMMYYY? OH MY GOD!'

I rolled my eyes at Swanny as if to say, 'I can't get a minute's peace these days.'

We turned around like film stars reluctantly greeting our public through gritted teeth. A man was running towards me. Jesus, I thought, this guy is really keen. He must be an absolute cricket nut.

He got closer. And closer still.

He reached me.

He kept running.

I turned round, confused. The comedian Jimmy Carr was standing about ten yards behind me, now posing for a photo.

CAPTAINS

Barry Johnston:

In October 1998, during the Second Test against Pakistan at Peshawar, the Australian captain Mark 'Tubby' Taylor tied Sir Donald Bradman's sixty-eight-year-old Australian Test record of 334 runs. Although the team voted for him to continue to bat the following morning, Taylor declared his side's innings closed after he had tied the record. The Don, who was then ninety years old, sent Taylor a telegram of congratulations.

Shortly afterwards in Australia a newspaper advertisement for toilet paper appeared. It read: 'Tubby, it's good to see you with the runs again!'

Dickie Bird:

A former Hampshire captain is Nick Pocock, who once played in a benefit match for Ken Barrington in Amsterdam, on a very hot day. He got quite a few runs, and when he came off the field, sweat was pouring out of him. His shirt was wet through. He wasn't too sure where the showers were, never having played on the ground before, but Surrey's Ron Tindall was quick to help.

'We've made arrangements,' said Ron, 'to shower in that house on the other side of the road. If you don't fancy a shower, you can have a bath.'

So Nick made his way over, undressed, helped himself to a whisky and settled down to soak in the bath. He had been luxuriating in the tub for a few minutes when, to his amazement, a woman walked in. Nick didn't know how to cover his embarrassment, and she was just as shocked as he was. 'What on earth do you think you are doing in my bath?' she demanded.

Nick stuttered, 'I'm playing in the cricket match across the road and we've been given permission to shower and bath here.'

The woman shouted for her husband, who stormed in red-faced. 'Who are you? I've given no one permission to shower, bath, drink my whisky or anything else. Now clear off before I call the police.'

When Nick returned to the pavilion, Tindall popped his head round the door and asked, 'Enjoy your shower, Nick?'

Brian Johnston:

There's a different sort of captain I rather like – Keith Miller, the jovial chap from Australia. A marvellous figure of a man. He loved hitting sixes, bowling bouncers and backing horses. He loved women and they loved him. He didn't worry much about tactics or laws, but he just enjoyed playing with his friends on, and off, the field.

There's a lovely story about him. He didn't captain Australia, but he captained New South Wales and he was leading them out once, walking twenty yards in front, a majestic figure, tossing his hair.

A chap called Jimmy Burke ran up and tugged his sweater and said, 'Nugget!' (He used to call him 'Nugget'.) 'Nugget, Nugget, we've got twelve men on the field!'

Miller didn't pause. He went walking on and said, 'Well, tell one of them to bugger off then!'

Graeme Fowler:

In my first season of opening regularly for Lancashire, I was batting with Clive Lloyd, when he called me down to him mid-over. It was getting to a stage where we needed to accelerate, and he was captain at the time, so I went down the wicket and asked, 'What?'

He looked down at me and said, 'My piles are killing me!' And he turned round and walked back.

I said to him afterwards, 'What on earth did you do that for?'

He said, 'Well, I thought you were looking a bit tense!'

Dickie Bird:

Keith Miller was one of the great Australian characters before and after the war. He was a bit forgetful at times, and one day the team was all set to take the field when Keith was asked, 'Where's old so-and-so?'

'No idea,' said Keith. 'Is he supposed to be playing?'

'Yes,' came the reply, '. . . and you were supposed to be giving him a lift!'

Simon Hughes:

In a knock-out match against Surrey at The Oval, the galumphing Sylvester Clarke produced a terrifying spell with the new ball, bulldozing through Middlesex's top order. The Middlesex captain Mike Brearley began the procession, getting out in the first over caught behind off a flier. His simmering mood was inflamed by Ted, the old Cockney attendant in the pavilion, saying innocently, ''Ere, Mike, wot you doin' back so early? Ain't they started yet?'

Brearley nearly wrapped the bat around him.

Henry Blofeld:

Colin Ingleby-Mackenzie was the flamboyant captain of Hampshire who led them to their first county championship in 1961. Hampshire's training diet in those days used to be 'wine, women and song'. Colin was once asked what time he liked his players to be in bed and he said, 'By nine.'

When someone said, 'Isn't that a bit early?' he replied, 'Well, play does start at eleven thirty!'

Dickie Bird:

New Zealand have not always been one of the strongest cricketing nations, but they have retained an ability to laugh at themselves. With his team in desperate straits on one tour of England, captain Ken Rutherford gave a perfect example of how a little bit of light-hearted repartee can deflect criticism, and lift the mood at a time of crisis.

He was asked by a journalist if he found it personally distressing to be captain of the New Zealand ship. Rutherford looked at the journalist, smiled, cupped a hand to his ear and said, 'Sorry, I didn't quite catch that. Did you say *ship*?'

Chris England: Balham to Bollywood

At my level, being a good captain is at least as much about having the ability to cajole people into giving up half a Sunday as it is about motivation, skill or tactics. This means that I often find myself pitted against the type of captain I fear becoming above all others – the passenger captain. He is alarmingly common in the cricketing circles in which I move, and his approach has too many similarities to my own for me to sleep easy at nights.

He is the captain who organises a team, and puts himself through all the torture that entails, because he knows he wouldn't ever get a game otherwise. Typically, he will begin his career by forging a side from a bunch of old college mates or work colleagues, fixing up the odd friendly here and there. Soon he will move on to building up a fixture list of more frightening proportions, until the team threatens to take over the entire summer.

He makes all the telephone calls, he makes all the teas. He frets all week about some dilettante who doesn't let him know whether he can play until the morning of the match. When the dilettante does finally withdraw, usually because otherwise he'll see his girlfriend for only six days in the week, the passenger captain knocks himself out ringing everyone he knows trying to get an eleventh man. He turns up at the pub at lunchtime, twitching and sweating, having just persuaded someone who lived across the corridor from him at university fifteen years ago and whom he hasn't seen since to turn out for his team.

He then spends a will-sapping three-quarters of an hour trying to hurry his team out of the pub to start the game. He goes out to do the toss with the opposing captain, which he loses, and then scuttles off to pad up, because nobody else wants to open the batting. Instead of having a couple of balls lobbed at him to get his eye in, he trots around trying to get someone to do the scoring, begging others to put down the Sunday paper and do a couple of overs' umpiring.

Some years ago we played against an archetypal passenger captain. It happened that the team I had managed to put together for the occasion had just one decent bowler, and he hadn't appeared by the time the match got under way. As it turned out, he had left my painstakingly detailed directions to the ground by the phone and then gone to a completely different ground on the other side of London where he vaguely remembered playing once. I thus was forced to open the bowling with someone who hadn't bowled in years, and wasn't really sure he could remember how to do it.

The umpires came out, followed by their openers. One, relaxed, swinging his arms, grinning, made his way to the non-striker's end with his pal the umpire. The other, the passenger captain, was wound tight as a coiled spring. His kit gleamed whiter than white – brand-new pads and gloves, an expensive, new, freshly linseeded and as yet unmarked bat, and, amazingly, given my bowling attack, a bright spanking white helmet with a grille.

Grub, my makeshift opening bowler, shuffled in to begin the innings. As he brought his arm over, the ball slipped from his grasp a split second too soon and looped gently twenty feet up into the sky. As it arced slowly down the pitch some giggling broke out in the field, but nothing disturbed the awesomely tense concentration of the passenger captain. He kept his eye on the ball all the way, brand-new bat paused at the top of his backlift, just telling himself to wait, wait, wait to see if he would need to play the ball.

At the last instant, he seemed to realise that if he continued like that, the ball was actually going to smack him right in the eye. Perhaps not trusting his new grille, he ducked. The ball dropped over and behind his crouching form and, descending almost vertically now, landed perfectly on the top of middle stump, dislodging a single apologetic bail.

As I watched the passenger captain trudge disconsolately back to the pavilion to spend the rest of the innings either scoring or umpiring while his team-mates read the paper, what could I think, except: 'There but for the grace of God . . .'

Ian Brayshaw:

Some suggest it is a mistake to appoint a bowler to captain a cricket team because he either bowls himself too little or too much. Legend has it that it was invariably a case of the latter when J.W.H.T. Douglas captained England. Bowlers in Douglas's teams were known to mutter to each other when a new batsman came in, 'You go on now and bowl him in, Mr Douglas . . . we'll come on later and bowl him out.'

One day Douglas had gone on for so long that one of them felt moved to approach him.

'Don't you think it's time we had a change in the attack, Mr Douglas?'

'You could be right,' came the reply. 'I'll have a go at the other end!'

Dickie Bird:

Brian Close was a great captain. He joined Somerset from Yorkshire in 1972 and provided the spark that was to ignite the county and turn them into a trophy-winning side. He proved inspirational with his fearless batting and fielding. He instilled discipline into the side and injected a new determination to succeed. The only problem with Closey was that nothing was ever his fault.

Once, at Trent Bridge, he went out to bat in a bid to avert a Barry Stead hat-trick. The scoreboard read 42 for 3. As he came out he had a quick word with the outgoing batsman, Richard Cooper. There was a hush as Stead came in to bowl, with nine men huddled round the bat. Ever the one to take the bull by the horns, Close aimed an almighty swipe at the hat-trick ball.

It was bold, brave and not as daft as it looked, because there was only one man, Nirmal Nannan, in the outfield. Unluckily for Close, although he made good contact, the ball seemed to be attracted like a magnet to Nannan's hands and the fielder took the catch. The ground erupted.

All was quiet, however, in the Somerset dressing room as the players waited for the inevitable explosion when Closey stormed in. Sure enough, he hurled his bat to the floor, glared at the unfortunate Cooper, and snarled, 'Bloody hell, lad, you said it were swingin', but you never said it were seamin' an' all!'

Martin Johnson:

There are many stories revolving around Brian Close's total belief in his own infallibility, the most quintessential of which was experienced by Peter Roebuck when Close was captain of Somerset. Roebuck, then right at the start of his career, was batting pretty well, unlike the veteran Close at the other end, who could barely lay bat on ball. At the end of an over Close wandered down the pitch for a chat, and Roebuck fondly imagined that he might just be in for a word of encouragement, if not praise.

'I don't know, lad,' sighed Close. 'Don't understand it. It's bloody unplayable at my end, but they're bowling complete rubbish to you!'

Dickie Bird:

Robin Marlar was the captain of Sussex between 1955 and 1959 and it has been somewhat unfairly suggested that, while players followed David 'The Rev' Sheppard out of faith, and 'Lord Ted' Dexter out of loyalty, they followed Marlar out of sheer curiosity.

John Barclay became captain of the side in 1981. Barclay was an Old Etonian, as you can probably tell by his remark following a difficult decision he had to make when G.D. Mendis was batting for Sussex. Barclay declared with Mendis on 97 not out and chasing his fifth century in six innings.

Said Barclay, 'Oh, I do hope he doesn't think I'm a swine and a cad!'

Roger Morgan-Grenville:

Over the years, a list has evolved of main differences between the work of a Test captain and the White Hunters cricket club captain, which goes something like this:

- The Test captain is normally accompanied on to the field by ten players. It would be unusual for one to be on the loo and one still on the A34 as the rest of the team took to the field.
- The Test captain doesn't suddenly run back to the pavilion to agree with his opposite number the interpretation of the lbw rule, the 'retire at fifty' convention, and exactly what time to put the tea urn on.
- It is not normal practice for the Test captain to have to promise his strike bowler an extra two overs providing he agrees to bat at number eleven . . .
- . . . neither does he have to put someone in at the top of the batting order simply because they are going out to supper in Marlborough and need to be

away by 5.30 at the absolute latest, otherwise their wife will strangle them.

- He very rarely has to call a halt to a bowler's over halfway through, on the basis that it is so bad, and so full of wides and no balls, that darkness is likely to fall before he completes it.

- He doesn't have to hide his three worst fielders in positions of no consequence . . .

- . . . or agree that the wicketkeepers will swap gloves at the halfway stage, otherwise he won't have enough bowlers to do the full number of overs.

- He doesn't have to wonder if that new bloke who came along at the last minute with the wealth manager is a proper cricketer (who should bat early and bowl often), or a friend from the Marketing Department who only came along for some fresh air, and had borrowed some kit off his son.

- He doesn't have to ask the opposition skipper if he can borrow a couple of fielders to cover for two of his own who haven't turned up, and are out of phone contact.

- And finally, he doesn't have to ask his opposite number to put a slow underarm bowler on for the last over, so that his wicketkeeper's ten-year-old son can have a safe and meaningful bat without having his block knocked off by a deranged psychopath.

Barry Johnston:

During a tour match in South Africa in early 1994, Merv Hughes was bowling to the South African captain, Hansie Cronje, who was hitting him all over the ground. After the ball had crossed the boundary rope for the umpteenth time, Merv finally lost his cool. The Australian fast bowler strode down the pitch, stood in front of Cronje and let out the most enormous fart.

Glaring at the South African captain, Merv snarled, 'Try hitting that for six!'

It was about five minutes before the players had stopped laughing and the game could continue.

Dickie Bird:

Chris Tavaré was the captain of Somerset for three years between 1990 and 1993. There is no way, however, that Tavaré can be included among the list of big-hitting crowd-pleasers who have graced the Somerset county grounds through the years.

Journalist Martin Johnson once revealed that he used to carry a box of pigeons by way of insurance, just in case the telephone lines went down. One day, he said, it backfired on him. He was strapping an account of a six-hour Tavaré innings on to the pigeon's back when he realised that the poor bird had fallen into a deep coma.

By the time he managed to revive it, the last edition of his paper had long gone!

John Barclay:

Middlesex v Sussex at Hove in 1980 – I toss up with Mike Brearley and win. Walking back to the pavilion to convey this news to the team, I was addressed by a lady at the boundary edge.

'Mr Barclay,' she said. 'Have you won the toss?'

'Yes,' I replied proudly.

'And are you going to bat?'

'Yes,' I said, even more proudly.

'And are you opening the batting?'

'Yes,' I said, puffing out my chest.

'In that case,' said the lady, 'I'll go into Hove to do my Sainsbury's shop before lunch!'

Dickie Bird:

I was still at school when I saw Walter Hammond play but I reckon he was probably the best player on all pitches who has ever lived. He played for Gloucestershire and England and, of course, he captained England.

For many years I umpired with Arthur Jepson – we were both on the first-class umpires list – and before that Arthur used to play for Nottinghamshire. He told me this story about a match he played in against Gloucestershire at Bristol. He said, 'It's a true story, Dickie, because I bowled at Hammond, so I know it's true.'

Walter Hammond won the toss and decided to bat first. He said to Charlie Barnett, 'I want you to go in first.'

Charlie said, 'I'm not going in first. I'll go in at number three when the shine's off the ball.'

Hammond said, 'I'm captain. If you don't open the innings, you can go home.'

So they had an argument and after that Charlie Barnett had to go in first. He got out to the last ball before lunch for 99. He came back to the dressing room, threw down his bat and said to Walter Hammond, 'That's how you bat, you so-and-so.'

After lunch Hammond went in at number three and between lunch and tea – Arthur Jepson told me he bowled at him all afternoon – Walter Hammond scored more than 200. He came into the pavilion at teatime and he said to Charlie Barnett, 'That's how you bat, Charlie. *That's* how you bat!'

Barry Johnston:

Before he became a popular Hollywood character actor in the 1930s, Sir C. Aubrey Smith was captain of Sussex for three years and he even played in one Test for England. He was known as 'Round the Corner' for his unusual bowling style and he was a founder-member of the Hollywood Cricket Club. He was playing cricket once in America when he dropped an easy catch and called for his butler to bring out his glasses. Soon afterwards he dropped another catch and exclaimed, 'The idiot brought my *reading* glasses!'

Later in his life Smith was very deaf and he was at a dinner party in Hollywood when the conversation around him became very animated. He guessed that they were talking about the merits of different sports, when in fact they were discussing homosexuality, and the other dinner guests were surprised when he suddenly remarked, 'Well, whatever you say, give me three stumps, a bat and a ball!'

TEST MATCH SPECIAL

Brian Johnston:

I was very lucky to get into *Test Match Special*. I did twenty-four years on the television up to 1970 and then they got fed up with all my bad jokes and thought they would get in some Test players to do the commentary, which was sensible, because they do it very well.

Luckily, I went straight into *Test Match Special* and it's a lovely programme to do, because we go and watch cricket like anyone else, with friends. If someone says, 'Have a little drink,' we might have a small one, or if someone has heard a good story, we might tell it. I hope we never miss a ball, but we have *fun* and that's the great thing to me about cricket.

We have got one or two eccentric people in the commentary box. What about Blowers, 'my dear old thing' – Henry Blofeld? When he was aged eighteen, Henry was one of the best wicketkeepers at Eton anyone had ever seen. He was captain of the Eton XI, but one day he rode a bicycle out of the playing fields into Datchet Lane and he was knocked over by a Women's Institute bus.

The ambulance took him away and he had an operation on his brain. He got a Blue at Cambridge later! So he was all right, but I think that accident gave him what I call 'busitis', because doing a commentary at Lord's he'll say, 'That ball goes through to the wicketkeeper. I can see a number eighty-two bus approaching . . . a Green Line bus . . . a double-decker bus . . .' He has buses on the brain! At The Oval once he said, 'I can see a good-looking bus!'

If a pigeon flies by, it's always 'a thoughtful-looking pigeon'. At Headingley, he said, 'I can see a butterfly walking across the pitch . . . and what's more, it's got a limp!'

He gets terribly excited. Someone dropped an easy catch and he said, 'A very easy catch. Very easy catch. It's a catch he'd have caught ninety-nine times out of a thousand!'

Henry Blofeld:

My first Test match in 1974 was not without incident because there was a lot of rain. You know how on *Test Match Special* we prattle on when it rains and we never hand back to the studio. We talk about absolutely anything. I was rather frightened about doing this at first, but Brian Johnston was marvellous at it. If there were forty-eight hours in a day, he would never have drawn breath and I don't know how he did it.

On the second day after lunch there was no play and Brian said, 'Let's bring Blowers in.' I'd thought of a few things to say, so I sat down and Johnners got up. I put my head to the windscreen, so to speak, and I started off. I rattled on for about ten minutes and I thought I was doing awfully well. I was telling them about this, that and the other, and I thought it was really sparkling stuff. Then I ran out of steam and I thought, goodness me, I need a bit of help.

So I stopped and looked to my right – I was sitting in the left-hand end of the box – and there should have been about four people there. To my absolute horror there was no one there at all. Not a soul. There was just a piece of paper almost in front of me in BJ's writing, and written on it was: CARRY ON UNTIL SIX-THIRTY AND DON'T FORGET TO HAND BACK TO THE STUDIO.

It was then about two-thirty.

Suddenly flat panic set in and I couldn't get any sense out at all. This seemed to go on forever until they all came tumbling back into the box, howling with laughter. But what Johnners had been saying to me in the nicest possible way, and doing it with great tact and humour, was, 'Hey, watch it, you're playing a team game,' and I never forgot that. It really taught me a lesson!

Peter Baxter:

There is a line in the film *Four Weddings and a Funeral*, which is spoken by Kristin Scott Thomas to Hugh Grant: 'There's a sort of greatness to your lateness.' It always make me think of CMJ – Christopher Martin-Jenkins.

I produced *Test Match Special* for thirty-four years, and shortly before I retired from the BBC, I received a call from CMJ on the morning of a match at The Oval. He said, 'I've gone to Lord's . . . where are you?'

On another occasion we were having a team photograph, as we tended to do every year. We were doing this one at Edgbaston. I had posted notices all around the commentary box to tell the commentators when it was going to happen, and Christopher arrived in time at ten o'clock in the morning on the Friday of the Test match.

He said, 'There you are, you're always telling me I'm late. Well, here I am.'

I told him, 'You're very early. We're doing it to-morrow.'

And the next day, he missed it!

Henry Blofeld:

Another thing that Johnners did during my first Test match nearly ended my entire broadcasting career. It's something I shall never forget. On one of the days when there was some cricket, Tony Greig was bowling to Sunil Gavaskar, the Indian opening batsman.

Johnners was on the air and he said, 'Here comes Tony Greig now from the Warwick Road End, this great gangling tall chap, he's up to the wicket now and he bowls and Gavaskar plays forward, and that one runs down to Hendrick at mid-on. Hendrick picks it up, looks at the ball, polishes it and throws it back to Greig, who now strides back down this long run of his, polishing the ball on his right thigh. He gets to the end of his run, he turns, sees Gavaskar is ready, and in he comes again. He's up there, he bowls, Gavaskar plays forward, and history repeats itself. The ball rolls down to Hendrick at mid-on, who picks it up this time and throws it straight back to Greig and now, to ring the changes as he walks back, Greig polishes his left ball.'

At which point the entire commentary box fell about, including dear old BJ, and the only thing he was able to say – it was the last ball of the over – was, 'and now, after a word from Trevor Bailey, it will be Henry Blofeld.'

The box was heaving, Frindall was snorting, and how I got through the next over I will never know!

Bill Frindall:

For several seasons Henry Blofeld relied on me to scrutinise any notes or emails that were passed to him. In fact,

I became his censor. Brian Johnston, David Lloyd, Jonathan Agnew, and even our producer, all competed in a prolonged campaign to get him to read out the most blatant *double entendres*. Frequently they have succeeded in bypassing me by slipping them under his pile of post from the far side, hidden under *bona fide* notes instructing him to hand over for the shipping forecast.

One slipped through the net just before lunch on a Saturday at Edgbaston and involved Evesham Cricket Club. The club asked us to pass an urgent message to their scorer, who was sitting in the Eric Hollies Stand. Apparently, his deputy had been taken ill and they needed him back.

The note advised that the scorer, Richard Head, would be listening to *TMS*. 'Dick's a shy man,' the note continued, 'and he wouldn't want to hear his name read out over the ground's public address system. Please help us get him back for our afternoon match.'

Blowers dutifully read out the note and added, 'So, if you're listening Dick Head, please hurry back to Evesham!'

Barry Johnston:

Brian was renowned for his practical jokes in the box, but his fellow commentators would occasionally get their own back. The stakes seem to have been raised when Jonathan Agnew joined the team as the new BBC Cricket Correspondent in 1991. The two of them usually broadcast at different times, which meant that any practical jokes required advance planning.

Neville Oliver was the popular Australian commentator, promptly renamed 'Dr NO' as soon as Brian saw his initials listed on the commentators' rota. During the 1993 Ashes series, Agnew recruited the Doctor to help him pull off a classic practical joke. They had received a list of the people who would be making the presentations on the pavilion balcony after the match. Agnew talked his idea over with the Doctor and then surreptitiously typed an additional name at the bottom of the list, photocopying the page to make it look more realistic.

Before the presentation ceremony he handed the paper over to Brian, who proceeded to read the list out on the air, including the surprise announcement that also present on the balcony was the managing director of the Cornhill Insurance Group, Mr Hugh Jarce!

Henry Blofeld:

I never commentated with Rex Alston, but his finest hour in the cricket world came in 1962 and it's hysterically funny. Whenever I feel badly in need of a glass of champagne and I haven't got one, I put on a tape of this, and it's jolly nearly as good.

In 1962 when Pakistan came to England for the second time, they had a player whose name was a commentator's nightmare. It was Afaq Hussain.

In those days, the commentary boxes for television and radio were on the first-floor balcony in the pavilion. Brian Johnston presided over television and Rex Alston was on the radio. Rex was always known as 'Balston', for the very simple reason that he got so many things wrong, and Johnners loved to pull his leg. So, about half an hour before the start, Johnners went into the radio box and said, 'Morning, Balston, I see Afaq's not playing.'

Rex said, 'Oh, Johnners, I wish you'd never mentioned his name. I shall never get it out of my mind all day.' But as he went out of the box, Johnners kept muttering, 'Afaq, Afaq.' Well, Rex tried awfully hard before lunch and he never thought about the name at all. He had a completely teetotal lunch, in order not to think about it before tea, but the problem started after tea. He was doing the final twenty-minute session of the day, there were about eight or nine minutes to go, and in his lovely modulated voice he said, 'England have had a really marvellous day here at Lord's. There has hardly been a cloud in the sky. Barry Knight is playing a very useful innings and I can tell you now that Javed Burki, the Pakistan captain, has made a gambler's last throw. We've got a change of bowling and we're going to see Afaq to Knight at the Nursery End . . . Oh! What am I saying? He's not even playing!'

Brian Johnston:

To me, John Arlott did more to spread the gospel of cricket than anybody. That marvellous Hampshire burr with the slightly gravel voice, especially in the years after the war, went all around the world, from igloos in Iceland to the outback in Australia.

Every time you heard him, you could smell bat oil and new-mown grass, and picture white flannels on a village green with a pub and a church. He could really conjure up cricket for you, and he was very good at painting a picture with words, because before he became a commentator, he was a poet.

To show you how quick he was, and how witty – one famous example happened when England were in South Africa in 1948/49. George Mann, the England captain, was clean bowled by 'Tufty' Mann, the South African slow left-hander, and John said, 'Another example of Mann's inhumanity to Mann!'

Fred Trueman:

John Arlott was never at a loss to find the right words to describe a situation for those who could not see it. Many of his descriptive phrases have passed into both broadcasting and cricket legend:

'Umpire Fagg, his face like Walt Disney's idea of what a grandfather should look like.'

On a characteristically long and dogged innings from Geoffrey Boycott: 'No man is an island, but he has batted as though he was a particularly long peninsula.'

'Dennis Lillee begins his run-up; black hair lounging on his shoulders like an anaesthetised cocker spaniel.'

'Bev Congdon remains at the crease to frustrate England, like some lingering, unloved guest at a party.'

Peter Baxter:

In the early nineties, Blowers went off to do a stint for Sky television and because we were getting so many letters asking, 'Where's Henry?', Brian Johnston said to me, 'We really ought to be saying something.' I was a bit pompous and said, 'No, I'm not going to give Sky a plug.' So Brian said, 'Don't worry, I shall be subtle.' And then I was really worried.

What he said was, 'People have been asking where old Blowers is. Well, he has gone to a place in the Sky.'

Next day, black-edged cards came pouring into the box saying, 'Deepest sympathy in your time of loss'!

Brian Johnston:

Luckily for me, I wasn't on air when the first streaker came on at Lord's. Remember the male streaker in 1975? He ran on and did the splits over the stumps. Fortunately, John Arlott was on and he described it brilliantly, wittily and gently. He said everything that needed saying; he didn't hide what he could see but he did it in a way that I couldn't possibly have done. I'd have got the sack, but he didn't.

It was interesting because Alan Knott was the non-striker at the far end. This chap came from the Pavilion End and did the splits over the stumps and then ran down towards the Nursery End. I said, 'What was it like out there, Knotty?'

'Oh,' he said, 'it really was most extraordinary. It's the first time I've ever seen two balls come down the pitch at the same time!'

Henry Blofeld:

John Arlott's choice of adjectives was supreme. 'The big, burly Bedser striding in from the Pavilion End' conjured up the perfect picture of a genial tidal wave, just as 'the balcony on the first floor of the pavilion with the portly iron railing' left one in no doubt as to the shape of this particular balcony at Old Trafford. It perfectly described a railing that bulges towards the base and looks like every elderly tummy one has ever seen.

It was at the Lord's Test match in 1975 that England's first streaker appeared, a merchant seaman from Marylebone who was enjoying his shore leave more than he should have done. Happily, Arlott was on the air most memorably to immortalise the moment:

We've got a freaker! Not very shapely . . . and it's masculine. And I would think it's seen the last of its cricket for the day. The police are mustered; so are the cameramen and Greg Chappell. He's being embraced by a blond policeman and this may be his last public appearance, but what a splendid one. He's now being marched down in a final exhibition past at least eight thousand people in the Mound Stand, some of whom, perhaps, have never seen anything quite like this before!

Brian Johnston:

There was a Yorkshireman who used to send me rhymes about cricket and he sent me one about the Lord's streaker:

> *He ran on in his birthday attire*
> *And he set all the ladies afire*
> *When he came to the stumps*
> *He misjudged his jumps*
> *Now he sings in the Luton Girls' Choir!*

Barry Johnston:

The Yorkshire-born cricket commentator Don Mosey, who was known as 'The Alderman', had one of the most distinctive voices on *TMS*. He was also the worst giggler in the commentary box and he shared with Brian Johnston an acute sense of the ridiculous that could swiftly reduce them both to helpless giggles. One day a listener sent in a copy of the Israeli Cricket Association's handbook. Brian was sitting at the back of the commentary box, flipping idly through the book, when he came to the record section. His eye fell on the pair who had made the highest tenth-wicket stand for Israel, Solly Katz and Benny Wadwaker.

He tried desperately not to make a noise, but soon stifled laughter exploded from the back of the box. Don Mosey was on air at the time and, without having any idea what was funny, found himself overcome by Brian's infectious high-pitched giggle and was completely unable to continue!

Peter Baxter:

A few years ago at Trent Bridge our commentary position, which had been in the pavilion for many years, moved to the other end of the ground after the new Radcliffe Road stand was built. It's a funny thing, because you spend a week in a commentary box in a Test match, looking out at the same skyline and it becomes very familiar. Suddenly, after years of one view from this ground, we were looking at it from a totally different angle. It was almost like being on a different ground as far as we were concerned in the commentary box.

Henry Blofeld was delighted. He was looking back at the old Victorian pavilion, but the best thing was that he could now see down the road into West Bridgford, where there were lots of buses. It was wonderful. He was having an absolute field day.

Then he realised that beyond the pavilion, on a hill, stood a rather good-looking church surrounded by trees. 'What a lovely church,' he said, 'it looks splendid up there.'

On the Friday afternoon, a column of smoke went up from the churchyard. 'That's good,' said Blowers, 'the vicar's having a barbecue. What a lovely vicar he must be, so kind to his parishioners.'

Two members of the cricket committee arrived in the commentary box in double-quick time to inform us that it was the Wilford Hill Crematorium!

Brian Johnston:

We have this funny thing in the commentary box about chocolate cake. It is silly, really, but someone sent me a cake once for my birthday and, perhaps unwisely, I said on the radio, 'Thank you very much for that delicious chocolate cake.'

Since then, they have arrived in droves. Of course, we played a silly trick on Alan McGilvray many years ago. Incidentally, I think Alan McGilvray was the least biased and the fairest of all commentators. He was very good and he knew his cricket, because he captained New South Wales in the 1930s, when people such as Jack Fingleton and Bill O'Reilly were under him, and Don Bradman on occasion.

So he knew his cricket, but he didn't always understand our jokes. At Lord's, I had cut some cake into slices on the desk alongside me and I was commentating when I saw him come in. I pointed to the cake and he nodded. I went on yap yapping away as he took a slice. 'That ball just goes off the edge of the bat and drops in front of first slip . . .' I watched Alan put the cake in his mouth and I said, 'We'll ask Alan McGilvray if he thought it was a catch.'

He went *pfffft*. There were crumbs everywhere!

BATTERS

Brian Johnston:

Denis Compton was the vaguest man there has ever been. He never remembered a single invitation, never arrived on time, always forgot his box or his bat or his pads, but went out and made a hundred with everybody else's equipment.

Many years ago Middlesex were giving a birthday party for him, on his fiftieth birthday. Champagne corks were popping in the Middlesex office up at Lord's when the telephone rang and they said, 'It's for you, Denis.'

He went, and came back looking a bit rum.

'Well, who was it, Denis?' they said.

'It's my mother,' said Denis. 'She says I'm only forty-nine!'

Dickie Bird:

The first West Indian batsmen to capture the public's imagination were the famous 'W' trio of Walcott, Weekes and Worrell. Jim Laker, that great England off-spin bowler, regarded Everton de Courcey Weekes as the greatest of the three, but was always curious about how he had come by his first name. One day he plucked up the courage to ask him.

'Ah, well, you see,' explained the West Indian, 'my dad was a football nutter. At the time I was born, Everton were the cock of the walk in the English First Division. So he decided to call me after that team.'

Said Laker, 'It's a bloody good job he wasn't a fan of West Bromwich Albion!'

Michael Parkinson:

Harold Larwood once told me of a famous encounter with Don Bradman at Leeds during the Third Test of the 1930 Ashes series when the little man played one of his great innings. Harold said there was no doubt in his mind that Bradman was the greatest batsman to whom he ever bowled.

'We worked on the theory he was uneasy against the short-pitched ball early on,' said Harold. 'Maurice Tate got Archie Jackson and they were two for one. I gave Bradman a short one first ball. He played at it and there was a nick. George Duckworth caught it. We thought we had him but the umpire didn't agree. Mind you, we got him out shortly after.'

'How many had he got?' I asked, walking blindfold into the trap.

'Three hundred and thirty-four,' replied Harold with a grin.

Ben Stokes:

My innings of 258 against South Africa in the second match of the series in January 2016 was the fastest score of 250 in Test history; I had registered the fastest double-hundred by an England player; the highest score ever by a number six; the 130 runs I contributed before lunch on day two was the most by a single player in a morning session; and no England player had struck as many as 11 sixes in one visit to the crease.

Sir Ian Botham said that I was a better player than him at the comparative age of twenty-four. All I can say is, he must have been drunk! Obviously it was a nice thing to hear, but I believe you achieve things across a career, not over three sessions of a Test match, so I don't tend to take anything from that kind of thing.

What I did take from the Cape Town match was a memento. I'm not particularly big on memorabilia for its own sake, but this was slightly different. I'm not sure whether I will get another Test double-hundred. So, after hands were shaken three days later, I made sure I grabbed one of the stumps and threw it into my kitbag. Later, I took out my Sharpie pen and wrote the details across the wood underneath Sunfoil, the sponsor's logo:

South Africa v England, Second Test,
Cape Town, 2–6 January 2016, 257

Yep, that's right. 257. I had written the wrong score down – in permanent marker ink! That's me, I guess: brilliant one minute, useless the next.

It took a fair old working over with an alcohol wipe to remove and correct it.

Martin Johnson:

In his early years with Leicestershire, there was no telling what kind of shambolic state David Gower would arrive in for breakfast, which led to his captain Ray Illingworth delivering him a 'smarten up' lecture. Gower's response was to turn up next morning wearing a dinner jacket and bow-tie, but Illy was not quite sure about the joke.

'Bloody hell, Gower,' he inquired. 'Have you just come in or are you just going out?'

Barry Johnston:

On 31 December 1920 a young woman named Mrs Park was sitting in the VIP enclosure at the Melbourne Cricket Ground, watching the Second Test match against England and happily doing her knitting. At one point, she fumbled and dropped her ball of wool. She bent down to pick it up – and missed her husband's entire international career!

Roy Park, known as 'Little Doc', was a doctor by profession. He played for Victoria and was making his Test debut, batting at number three for Australia. He was bowled first ball by Harry Howell, who was also making his Test debut. Australia went on to win the match by an innings and 91 runs, so Park did not face another ball, and was never selected again. Years later he admitted he hadn't been to bed the night before the Test because he had been supervising a difficult birth.

The good Dr Park was bowled by the only ball he ever faced in international cricket!

Simon Hughes:

There are as many Geoffrey Boycott stories as he's played forward defensives, but this is my favourite. Mike

Hendrick had been bowling some dastardly leg-cutters at our Geoffrey, none of which he could lay a bat on, but he kept up a gibing banter for most of the morning.

Hendrick (after an edge had gone between the slips): 'How many great bowlers *are* there in the world?'

Boycott (defiant): 'One less than tha thinks there are. Now, get back and bool.'

Hendrick (later, beating the bat): 'Has that bat got 'ole in it?'

Boycott: 'I'd put thee in mook and nettles if tha give me woon to reach.'

At length the mischievous umpire, Arthur Jepson, had had enough of this incessant rabbit and when Hendrick nipped one back into Boycott's pads and let out a half-hearted appeal, Jepson gave him out. Stunned and appalled by what appeared to be an outrageous injustice, Boycott marched off, muttering to the umpire as he passed, 'Hey, Arthur, what's happened to your guide dog?'

'I sacked it for yapping, same as I'm doing to you,' Jepson replied. 'Now piss off!'

Christopher Martin-Jenkins:

I love the relatively humble County Championship. These days there are sadly fewer first-class games than there once used to be, there are fewer grounds used, there is less variety, and therefore some of the character has gone out of the game. I think county cricket is at its very best on smallish grounds in smallish towns, rather than the big cities with the echoing stadiums. But strange things used to happen there.

I was in Ebbw Vale in the mining district of Wales, where Emrys Davies of Glamorgan was batting on one of those damp pitches. Batsmen always used to have a bit of mud on the back of their bat, from where they would pat the ground down. Emrys Davies had gone up to do that, when he went over to speak to his opening partner Gilbert Parkhouse in some alarm.

'Do you know,' he said, 'when I patted the ground just now, I could swear I heard some tapping coming up from underneath!'

Brian Johnston:

When Bryan 'Bomber' Wells came in to bat for Nottinghamshire against the Australians at Trent Bridge in 1964, Neil Hawke was in devastating form. The umpire, ready to give him guard, said, 'What do you want, Bomber?'

To which Bomber replied, 'Help!'

A few years earlier, when Bomber was playing for Gloucestershire, he was batting one day with Sam Cook. They got into a terrible tangle over a short single, with

Sam just making the crease by hurling himself flat on the ground. As he lay there panting he shouted out to Bomber, 'Call!'

Bomber shouted back, 'Tails!'

Colin Ingleby-Mackenzie:

I had entertained Denis Compton to lunch during a Test match at Lord's. After lunch we strolled round the ground and behind the pavilion we noticed Geoffrey Boycott and David Gower in a keen discussion. They were discussing how many first-class hundreds each had made. Geoffrey said, 'I told you I've made more than you!'

Denis Compton quickly retorted, 'And thank God I've only seen three of them!'

Michael Parkinson:

The Don Bradman legend is built on stories underlining the prowess that set him apart from other men. There is, for instance, the tale of Bill Black, an off-spin bowler playing for Lithgow, in New South Wales, who on a memorable day in 1931 bowled Bradman for 52. The umpire was so excited that when the ball hit Bradman's wicket he called out, 'Bill, you've got him!'

The ball was mounted and given to Bill Black as proof that he dismissed the greatest batsman in the world.

Later that season Don Bradman again played against Bill Black. As the bowler marked out his run, Don said to the wicketkeeper, 'What sort of bowler is this fellow?'

The wicketkeeper, a mischievous fellow, like the rest of his tribe, replied, 'Don't you remember this bloke? He bowled you out a few weeks ago and has been boasting about it ever since.'

'Is that so?' said Bradman.

Two overs later Black pleaded with his skipper to be taken off. Bradman had hit him for 62 runs in two eight-ball overs. He made a hundred in three overs and finished with 256, including 14 sixes and 29 fours!

The other side to Bradman's genius is demonstrated by an encounter with George Macaulay, the feisty Yorkshire seam bowler, in 1930. It was Bradman's first tour of England and there was a popular rumour that the English wickets would sort him out. As an ardent subscriber to this theory, Macaulay couldn't wait to get at Bradman.

When Yorkshire played the Australians early in the tour, Macaulay demanded loudly of his captain, 'Let me have a go at this bugger.'

His first over was a maiden. Bradman then hit him for five fours in the second over and took 16 from the third. A spectator yelled, 'George, tha' should have kept thi' bloody trap shut!'

Andrew Flintoff:

During the First Test against the West Indies at Lord's in 2004, there was a comical moment with my old friend Tino Best. We had got off to a bad start earlier that year in the Caribbean when he played a trick on me in the Second Test at Trinidad, which I didn't find very funny.

I had just walked out to bat and took guard ready for him to run in. He came charging in, like he does, and bowled and at first I thought it must have been a beamer, because I didn't see it come out of his hand. I was expecting to get hit on the head at any moment because I just hadn't picked it up. But he thought it was a huge joke, because he had run in without a ball in his hand. I'm the first one to enjoy a laugh and a joke on the field and there are some things you can do, but that was just not one of them. I didn't find it funny at all.

Four months later it was payback time at Lord's. I was standing at slip and Tino was trying to hit Ashley Giles out of the ground and swiping and missing. I couldn't help myself saying, 'Mind the windows, Tino!' And he just couldn't resist. He had to try to smash Giles again and of course missed altogether. The ball went straight through to wicketkeeper Geraint Jones and Tino was stumped by a mile.

Now that *was* a good laugh!

Barry Johnston:

The South African batsman Daryll Cullinan developed a phobia about playing against the leg-spin bowling of Shane Warne, who always seemed to get him out cheaply. In fact, before the South Africans toured Australia in 1997, there was an article in an Australian newspaper in which Cullinan revealed that he had seen a psychiatrist to help him overcome his fear of Shane Warne and the Aussies. Warne couldn't believe it.

The day of the First Test at Melbourne finally dawned. Adam Bacher fell to a fine slip catch by Mark Taylor and Cullinan walked out gingerly to the crease. Warne let him take guard before saying, 'Daryll, I've waited so long for this moment and I'm going to send you straight back to that leather couch.' A couple of balls later Warne bowled him for a duck. Cullinan was more embarrassed than anything else, but those words had clearly unsettled him, and he took no further part in the Test series.

However Cullinan got his revenge eighteen months later. During their 1999 World Cup encounter at Headingley, Warne again welcomed the unfortunate Cullinan to the crease by saying that he had been waiting months for the joy of renewing their acquaintance. This time Cullinan replied quickly, 'Yeah, and it looks like you've spent most of that time eating!'

Martin Johnson:

Ray Illingworth had a belief in his own ability that would occasionally have people in fits of helpless giggles. He was, for instance, never out when he was batting. On one occasion, having missed a particularly horrible slog, he returned to the dressing room and claimed that the bowler's grunt in his delivery stride made him think it was the umpire calling a no-ball. On another, when there seemed no possible excuse even for him, he said, 'Would you believe it? Bloody umpire gave me t'wrong guard.'

His reputation as a captain was for erring on the defensive side, which was again in keeping with his thrifty nature. He knew all the best fish and chip shops in Yorkshire, and which bars in Torremolinos gave you non-watered-down rum at the cheapest prices. Once, as captain of Leicestershire, he negotiated 10 per cent off the team's hotel bill, because he couldn't get any sausages for breakfast!

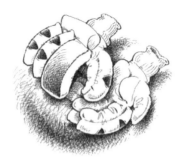

Dickie Bird:

Out of all the great players I've seen, if I had to pick a batsman to bat for my life, I'd go for Geoffrey Boycott. He was probably the best self-made player in the history of the game. Mind you, there were times in Test matches when I was umpiring and he was batting and he was there, blocking every ball, and I had to say to myself, 'Come on, get a grip of yourself, Dickie. Get a grip. Don't let him put you to sleep!'

I was told once that to make the best Yorkshire pudding you had to have a very slow batter – and Boycott springs immediately to mind.

Boycott had one bad habit – he ran people out. Me included. He once ran me out playing for Barnsley and I'd have had the biggest collection they'd ever had at Barnsley Cricket Club. I was on 49, there were three thousand people in the ground, and I hit this ball to deep midwicket. I shouted, 'Come two,' and ran down the pitch, and Boycott said, 'Keep running . . . into the pavilion!'

One man ran Boycott out. It was in a Test match in New Zealand. The England captain, Mike Brearley, had returned home with a broken arm and Geoffrey Boycott had been appointed as captain. England were playing New Zealand at Christchurch and the New Zealand captain left England a very good declaration. Bob Willis, the England vice-captain, called a meeting in the England dressing room as Boycott and Brian Rose were padding up to go out and open the innings for England.

Bob Willis said, 'Lads, we're going for these runs because we can win this Test match. This is a tremendous declaration. Now then, Geoffrey, I want you to play a few shots.'

Boycott said, 'Huh! I shall play me own game. Ain't nobody gonna tell me how I'm gonna play. I shall be 120 not out at close of play.'

Bob Willis said, 'I want you to get out there and get on with it, because we can win this Test match.'

Boycott and Rose went out and opened the innings for England. Brian Rose was out after about an hour and Derek Randall went in next, but Boycott had put England well behind the clock. So Bob Willis called another meeting in the England dressing room. He said, 'Gentlemen, I want a volunteer to pad up and go in next, if Randall gets out, and run Boycott out!'

Ian Botham said, 'I volunteer!'

He said, 'Right, Both. If Randall gets out, you go in next.'

Well, Randall got out and Botham went in, and as he left the England dressing room all the England lads said, 'Good luck, Both!'

He said, 'Leave it to me.' Botham got out to the middle and he had a meeting with Boycott. He said, 'Geoffrey, instructions from the England dressing room: you have put us well behind the clock and you've got to play a few shots. You've got to get on with it.'

'I shall play me own game. There's no one telling me how I'm gonna play.'

Botham said, 'I'm telling you.'

'Well, there's nobody's telling me. I shall be 120 not out.'

Botham said, 'Oh, will you?'

Botham got down to face his first delivery. In came the bowler, Botham pushed the ball to cover point and shouted to Boycott, 'Come one!' Boycott, head down, charged down the wicket and nearly reached Botham's end, but Botham was still sat on his bat. He said, 'Sorry, Geoffrey, I'm not coming.' Boycott turned, tried to get back, but was run out by half the length of the field.

Boycott has hardly spoken to Botham since that day!

Fred Trueman:

In his old age, Sir Donald Bradman retained a wicked sense of humour. He was once asked by a newspaper-man, 'How do you think you would have fared against today's bowlers, Sir Donald? Your career average was ninety-nine in Tests; what do you think it would have been against modern bowling and field-placing?'

Bradman pondered the point for a moment, then replied, 'I think I might have averaged about thirty-eight or thirty-nine perhaps.'

The reporter was shaken. 'Do you mean,' he asked breathlessly, 'that you regard today's bowling as so much better?'

'Oh, no,' said Sir Donald. 'What you asked was what do I think I would have averaged *today*, and the answer is thirty-eight or thirty-nine. Don't forget that *today* I'm eighty-four years old!'

Richie Benaud:

I like the story about Colin Cowdrey when he was flown out to Australia as an additional batsman in 1974, after Dennis Amiss and John Edrich suffered broken bones in the First Test in Brisbane.

In the Second Test at the WACA in Perth, Cowdrey batted number three and went in after Brian Luckhurst was caught by Ashley Mallett in the gully off Max Walker for 27, with the score 44. It was a perfect day and 16,000 spectators watched Cowdrey walk to the centre. The crowd was lively, because they were watching some very fast bowling from Jeff Thomson and Dennis Lillee. No one said a word to Colin.

After a couple of overs, as 'Thommo' was walking back past the non-striker's end, Colin took a pace towards him, smiled and said politely, 'Good morning, my name's Cowdrey!'

Sometimes you need a sense of humour. In the same

game David Lloyd made 49 in the first innings and announced to his fellow players that he could play Thomson with his prick. In the second innings he had made 17 when Thommo got one to rear and the ball smashed his protective box to pieces. When they had airlifted him back to the England dressing room, his first agonising words through gritted teeth to solicitous teammates were, 'See, told you I could!'

TALES FROM INDIA

Brian Johnston:

I went to India for the first time in 1993 to commentate on England's Test matches in Madras and Bombay. It is a very strange country. In fact, I still don't know whether they drive on the left or the right. They steer very well, even around the cows lying in the middle of the road, but it is all very frightening.

And, of course, the food is very tricky, but they have got a new dish especially for Englishmen. It's called Boycott curry. You still get the runs, but more slowly!

Barry Johnston:

Indian cricket fans love their cricket, but they also hate losing. When India were only a few wickets from defeat in their 1996 World Cup semi-final against Sri Lanka, the crowd at Eden Gardens in Kolkata became increasingly restless, throwing bottles, cans and plastic bags onto the field. After they started to burn down the stands, the match had to be abandoned and it was awarded to Sri Lanka.

So when India lost three ODI series in a row the following year under the captaincy of Sachin Tendulkar, the Indian team were rightfully worried for their safety. All the players locked themselves in their homes for a few days, not daring to go outside because they were fearful of being attacked.

There was a popular story at the time about the Indian fast bowler Javagal Srinath. After staying inside his house for a week, his wife pestered him to go to the market to buy some groceries.

'I can't,' he said. 'It's too dangerous.'

'Then shave off your moustache and wear one of my sarees,' his wife said. 'No one will recognise you.'

So Srinath shaved off his moustache, put on his wife's clothes and went down to the busy market. He had nearly finished his shopping and so far nobody had recognised him: his wife's plan had worked. He was collecting his change from the shopkeeper, when a short lady wearing a burqa walked up alongside him and whispered, 'How are you doing, Srini? I haven't seen you in a while.'

'Who are you?' said Srinath, shocked. 'How did you recognise me?'

'Don't worry,' hissed the young lady from behind her burqa. 'It's me . . . Sachin Tendulkar!'

Graeme Fowler:

It was the third day of the Third Test against India at Calcutta, January 1985. Boring Shastri, boring Azharuddin. Both got centuries, which seemed their main concern, but on the flattest, most placid wicket imaginable. We kept ourselves amused by fooling around. Our entertainments ranged from fielding in police hats, acrobatics, conducting the crowd's cries of 'We want Kapil', to throwing in rubber balls. Anything to make a dull day pass more quickly, but also to wake us up.

Then 151 overs into the match, our all-rounder, Chris Cowdrey, came on to bowl. He also provided the high-light of the day. After tea he had Mike Gatting at first slip. David Gower said, 'Do you want Gatt a foot wider?'

'No,' said Cowdrey, 'he'd burst!'

Sachin Tendulkar:

In April 1998 we went to Sharjah for yet another tri-series, with Australia and New Zealand. It is a tournament I remember well because I played some of my best cricket then, and because of an incident that took place on the flight out to Sharjah.

The Indian team included two relative newcomers, Harbhajan Singh and Harvinder Singh, the medium-fast bowler. The flight attendant asked both of them if they wanted soup. Not very good with English at the time, Harvinder may not have understood the question. I overheard Harvinder tell Bhajji that it was prudent just to take what was being served.

Then Harvinder, trying to figure out what to add to his soup, ended up adding sugar-free sweetener instead of salt. He was too embarrassed to admit his mistake and so he pretended to like it.

Bhajji, who always enjoyed a laugh, was aware of what Harvinder had done and kept asking him if he was enjoying his food!

Miles Jupp:

While I was at the First Test against India at Nagpur in 1993, several local newspapers carried a story about an English cricket fan who had visited one of Nagpur's restaurants one evening. In addition to sampling the local cuisine, he had also poured enough wine and beer down his neck to sedate all of the members of the Happy Mondays. He had somehow managed to return to his hotel, and once there he realised that he was no longer sure of the whereabouts of the camera that he was certain he had brought with him to the restaurant earlier in the evening.

Instead, however, of then chalking it up as a casualty of drinking and then sensibly passing out in a pool of his own effluent, he returned to the restaurant and accused two waiters of stealing his camera. Then he called the police to report them, before returning once more to his hotel.

So far, so undignified. But then two mornings later the man had been going through his luggage and happened upon his missing camera in, as the paper told me, 'the pocket of his Bermuda'. To his credit, our English friend immediately got in touch with the police to inform them of his error, but the Indian legal system had already leapt into action with surprising alacrity in response to his inebriated finger-wagging; the waiters had been arrested, and were appearing in court that very morning.

Thus the accuser had to turn into a saviour, and made it to the courthouse just in time to sign an affidavit stating that the two hapless waiters were not responsible for the imagined theft. They were granted bail, and the English cricket fan who had brought the camera to the court with him to prove that it had not in fact been stolen, then had his camera confiscated by the police!

Matthew Hayden:

On the 2004 tour of India in October, the Australian team stayed at the Pride Hotel in Nagpur for the Third Test. Downstairs in the main buffet of the hotel, some of the boys were having lunch when a cockroach popped its head up out of the middle of a rogan josh and started to run for safety. A waiter heard the groans of Gilchrist, Kasprowicz and Ponting and swiftly grabbed the insect and – for reasons we still haven't got to the bottom of – put it in his mouth.

'A cockroach!' was the collective cry from the boys.

The waiter shook his head, 'No, sir, no cockroach.'

The boys were having none of it. 'It's a cockroach!' they protested, to the waiter's further denials.

'Fair enough, then,' said one of the boys finally. 'If it's not a cockroach, then eat it.'

And the waiter did!

Christopher Martin-Jenkins:

The passion for cricket in India doesn't change. When I first went to India, there were huge crowds to watch three-day games between such exotic-sounding teams as

Indian Universities against MCC. Never was there a day's play on that tour when there was not a full house. Now they have switched their allegiance to the short form of the game, but the Indians remain great players and they are still passionate supporters.

On tours to the subcontinent, they last a long time and you need characters in the cricket team, no less than in the press and media parties. One of the unsung ones of relatively recent times was Dean Headley, who was a terrific-hearted fast bowler. On one of those trips by air from one cricketing town to another, he was battling with a general knowledge crossword and he called across to me in his Brummie accent, 'Here, CMJ, you're intelligent, you'll know the answer to this one: "Seven wonders of the world". Is it the Hanging Baskets of Babylon?'

Barry Johnston:

Sachin Tendulkar now features regularly in the *Forbes* list of the ten richest celebrities in India, thanks to the returns on his investments and his brand endorsements, but he once stunned a bank official who was trying to encourage the young Indian batsman to take out a credit card. After writing down Sachin's name and address and other personal details, the bank manager came to the next question on his list.

'Mr Tendulkar, do you earn more than 300,000 Rupees (£3,000)?'

Tendulkar shrugged his shoulders and said, 'Some days yes and some days no!'

Peter Baxter:

My first overseas production was in India at a place called Ahmedebad. On this occasion we should have been commentating on an ODI between England and India, but we couldn't get on the air and nothing was happening. There was absolute silence on the line. Meanwhile Christopher Martin-Jenkins was having to play music from the BBC studio back in London to fill the dead air.

I was sitting there with headphones clamped to my ears, calling out, 'Hello, London! Hello, Bombay! Hello anyone beyond Ahmedebad!' but nothing was happening.

Suddenly, in the far distance, I could hear this very faint voice.

'*Hello, hello?*'

It was wonderful.

I said, 'Hello, Bombay. Put me through to London.'

The voice said, '*Hello, hello?*'

I said, 'Come on, Bombay, we should have been on the air an hour ago. Put me through to London!'

The voice kept saying, '*Hello, hello?*'

At this point, one of the other commentators tapped me on the shoulder, and pointed to a Sikh engineer, who was sitting right behind me, talking into a telephone.

'Hello, hello?'

We were on air later than expected that day.

Barry Johnston:

In the winter of 1937/38, there was no England Test tour, so Lord Tennyson led an MCC team on a five-month tour of India. It was a first-class team, including several top England and county players. They sailed to Bombay on the luxury liner *The Viceroy of India* and then travelled by train across the subcontinent and around the coast by ship, staying mainly in the local maharajah's palace or in top-class hotels.

In those days the visiting teams played a number of matches up-country before their first Test against India. Early on in the tour, Lord Tennyson's XI were playing against the Rajputana XI at Ajmer in Rajasthan, northwest India. Unfortunately there was a severe outbreak of dysentery in the area and some members of the MCC team soon began to feel unwell, including the Surrey fast bowler Alf Gover.

However, on the morning of the match, Gover assured his captain that he was fit enough to play. The Indians were batting, so Tennyson handed Gover the new ball and he paced out his long run-up down by the sight-screen.

He turned to bowl the first ball, but halfway towards the stumps he felt an ominous movement in his bowels. Alf kept on running, only slightly faster now, straight past the umpire, down the pitch and past the startled batsman at the other end.

'Where are you going?' shouted Tennyson.

'To the loo,' gasped Gover. 'Sorry, I can't stop!' and he disappeared into the pavilion.

Later one of the team asked Alf if he had made it in time.

'Nearly,' said Alf. 'I lost by two yards!'

When Gover had not returned after a few minutes, Lionel Tennyson sent the fielder at third man to find out what was going on.

The player entered the team dressing-room and knocked nervously on the lavatory door.

'Alf, is that you in there?' he said.

'Yes . . . it is,' came the feeble reply.

'What do you think you're doing?'

'Well, I've got an upset tummy,' groaned Alf.

'I can tell that,' said the fielder. 'But can we have our ball back!'

*Matthew Engel (from Wisden Cricketers'
Almanack 2016):*

Sachin Tendulkar sparked a social media frenzy in 2015 when he had dinner in an Oxfordshire village after watching Andy Murray at Wimbledon. He posted pictures of himself by a bus stop with the words, 'In Great Haseley, Oxfordshire. Missed the last bus, can anyone give me a lift?'

He was bombarded with messages from adoring fans either offering to help or apologising that they couldn't – mainly because they were in India. One claimed to have arrived to look for him.

Tendulkar was indeed in Great Haseley, but he had travelled by car. Two days later, he reposted the same pictures, overwritten with the words, 'Some seem to have missed the joke.'

One respondent said, 'God-level sarcasm is obviously difficult to understand for us humans!'

Peter Baxter:

The best stories do seem to come from India. There was a bus ride that we took from Kolkata to Jamshedpur, a little jaunt of about ten hours through the dark in West Bengal, when somewhere in the middle of nowhere, our press bus was held up by a tree trunk across the road. Bandits surrounded the bus.

We had a tour courier on the bus with us, a little man called Raju, who claimed to have the blood of the Rajput princes in his veins; he said his uncle was a Maharajah. So we sent him down the steps of the bus to go and negotiate with these cut-throats, and we shut the door behind him. There was a certain amount of animated conversation outside, before the door opened again, Raju got back on the bus, the tree trunk was moved and we carried on.

We were all wide awake by now, having been dozing before this, and we said, 'Raju, what's happening? How did you save our lives? What did you tell them?'

He answered grandly, 'I told them to bugger off!'

Vic Marks:

John Thicknesse was the *Evening Standard*'s cricket correspondent for thirty years. By the time I joined the pack in 1990, he was an accomplished, canny tourist.

In India, for example, in the days when cigarette smoking was widespread in the press corps and everywhere else, John always took the precaution of buying a cheap local packet on arrival; he would empty the contents and replace them with the treasured duty-free cigarettes of much higher quality that he had purchased at Heathrow Airport. In those days, it was appropriate to 'flash the ash' whenever lighting up, but no one ever took any of John's 'Indian' cigarettes!

John could be formidable at press conferences. Before England's tour to India in 1992, he challenged the chairman of selectors, Ted Dexter, about the controversial omission of David Gower.

'How is it, Ted, that you are setting off for India without a single Test-quality left-hander in your squad?'

Dexter spotted a rare half-volley from Thicknesse and with a gentle, triumphant smile, replied, 'Thickers, I think you'll find that Lancashire's Neil Fairbrother is in the squad.'

This provoked a firm and immediate response from Thicknesse.

'I said "Test-quality", Ted!'

Matthew Hayden:

I visited India many times as a player for Australia, but I must confess to being largely ignorant of the nuances of its different cultures, languages and dialects, and the fact that they could change every few hundred kilometres. I didn't realise there was no quintessential India or Indian, or that on any given day there could be eight different languages apart from English spoken in the Indian dressing-room.

My re-education often came in subtle ways. When I started playing for the Super Kings in the IPL, there were times when I'd be watching television with four or five Indian team-mates in our team room in Chennai, and one of them would start laughing at something said on television.

'What's he laughing at?' I'd say to one of the others, and he'd shrug and say, 'Don't know . . . not sure what dialect it is. We can't understand it either!'

Sachin Tendulkar:

One incident I remember from the Cape Town Test in 1997 – and one I thoroughly enjoyed – involved Allan Donald and the Indian medium-fast bowler Dodda Ganesh. Donald, who was in top form in that series, had no patience with lower-order batters and was frustrated to see Ganesh hanging around. As Dodda faced his onslaught fearlessly, Allan started mouthing words at him.

For three consecutive deliveries, Dodda was all over the place, but luckily for him did not lose his wicket. At the end of the over, Allan went up to Dodda and told him what he thought of him in no uncertain terms.

Dodda's face remained impassive.

I witnessed all this from the non-striker's end. When Allan came to collect his cap from the umpire, I told him, 'Allan, Dodda only knows a local Indian language called Kannada. I find it difficult enough to communicate with him myself, so how can he understand your abuse in English? If you want to get to him, you'll have to speak to him in Kannada.'

This made Allan even more irritated. He almost snatched his cap from the umpire and, making wild gestures with his hands, stomped off to his fielding position!

Miles Jupp:

The real fun in Chandigarh started when I attempted to log on to the hotel's wireless network. The signal was incredibly slow in the rooms, and continued to cut out every few minutes. Aggers kindly informed me that the signal was rather stronger out on the landing, so I took my laptop from my room and joined him and three or four other journalists, who were sitting there cross-legged on the floor. I was instantly able to post my blog, and then started to have a rummage through all of my emails and browsed the internet. All around me, the others tapped away, and some journalists disappeared and some new ones took their place.

At one point, a small fleet of hotel staff arrived to turn down everybody's beds and to scatter rose petals on them. Most of the doors were wide open, as if we were the cast of *Friends* enjoying another kooky night in together. One door was shut, and a member of staff knocked gently on it for nearly a minute. He was just about to slip his master key in the slot when the door opened and the man was startled to see Ian Botham appear before him looking like a sleepy Falstaff. The man was so startled that at first he did nothing, but just stood staring at Botham.

'Hello?' Botham said eventually, in order to break the silence.

'Your bed, sir?'

'My bed?'

'I'm to prepare your bed, sir. For sleeping.'

'It's okay. I'm already sleeping.'

'Are you sure, sir?'

'Yes. Really. It's fine.'

But the man was incapable of absorbing the information, or perhaps of just turning his back on a legend like the one before him. I don't know if there's an official record for 'longest time taken to convince hotel staff member that one's bed simply does not need to be turned down', but it seems unlikely that it has ever taken anyone longer to communicate or understand this fact. This bizarre stand-off lasted for an age, all the time Botham's face becoming all the more hangdog and his eyes narrowing in despair. Eventually, Botham closed the door.

The man stood there, still thinking. Then in a last-ditch attempt, he leant towards the door and shouted, 'Are you sure, sir? What about chocolates?'

Barry Johnston:

When he was sixteen years old and at the West Delhi Cricket Academy in 2005, Virat Kohli was made the captain of the Delhi Under-17 side. It was a club match and a young bowler from Najafgarh had also been selected for the team; he was new at the academy and Kohli had not played with him before.

Cricketers often use a kind of shorthand to save time, so instead of the captain asking a bowler, 'From which end do you want to bowl,' they will simply ask, 'From where?'

When it was the new player's turn to bowl, Virat Kohli went up to him and asked, 'From where?'

The young bowler replied, 'Najafgarh.'

'No,' said Kohli again, 'from *where?*'

The bowler gave the same reply, 'Najafgarh!

Stumped, Kohli had to explain to the young novice exactly what he meant.

Now one of the best batters of his generation, Virat Kohli says that he told this story to MS Dhoni while they were playing for India against Australia at Kolkata in 2017 – and the Indian wicketkeeper couldn't stop laughing!

CHARACTERS

Henry Blofeld:

Colin Milburn, known to everyone as 'Ollie', was in the same league as P.G. Wodehouse's Right Honourable friend who looked as if he had been poured into his clothes and had forgotten to say 'When!' Fat men are often naturally humorous and Milburn always seemed to be the ideal chap to audition for the job of Stan Laurel's partner if ever another had been needed.

Milburn's figure raised a few eyebrows when he first joined Northamptonshire. They sent him on training runs with the rest of the team, but he was just not built to run a long way. After about half a mile the others had left him behind, so he thumbed a lift on a milk float and sailed past the rest of the team a bit farther up the road!

On another occasion, Keith Andrew, his county captain, suggested that Colin should try to do something about his weight, and also get some more hundreds.

'Why don't you drink halves instead of pints?' Andrew asked. Milburn made 150 that day and it was only about halfway through the afternoon.

'What are you going to drink then, Colin?' Andrew asked him.

Quick as a flash he said, 'Two halves, please, guv!'

Fred Trueman:

Charles Bowmar Harris was well into the veteran stage when I first encountered him – he was over forty. I was under twenty – but I knew *of* him, of course, as everyone in the game knew of the practical joker and genial eccentric who had been Nottinghamshire's opening batsman since 1928.

Jim Laker used to tell how Charlie stopped a fast bowler in full cry in his approach to the wicket with the explanation, 'You have an extra fieldsman in the gully.' The whole game was held up for an investigation to be made and it was then discovered that Harris had placed his false teeth on the ground in roughly the place gully would stand.

No one escaped Charlie's droll humour – and no one resented it. One day he was batting against Surrey when he put a dolly catch into the air. As three fieldsmen plus wicketkeeper edged forward – all with an equal chance of making the catch – Charlie trotted gently by and shouted, 'Mine!' Everyone stopped . . . and the ball fell gently to earth!

Henry Blofeld:

Ollie Milburn came as a breath of fresh air for English cricket and it was cruel that, after playing in only nine Test Matches for England, he was involved in a car crash in 1969 that cost him the use of one eye and damaged the other. For a time he tried bravely to overcome this enormous handicap and his humour never left him.

He was playing against Derbyshire with only one eye and was bowling. As he ran in to deliver one ball, he suddenly stopped and shouted that his eye had fallen out. Everyone searched around the crease and the umpire found it. Milburn took out his handkerchief, gave the glass eye a rub, shoved it back in and, after a good chortle, finished the over.

Brian Johnston:

Brian Close was one of the bravest cricketers I've ever seen. Remember him batting against the West Indies in 1963, against Hall and Griffith? Rather than risk giving a catch, he bared his breast at them and let the ball hit him. You could see the maker's name all over him. He was very brave and, of course, he always fielded near in at short leg.

There's a story about when Yorkshire were playing Gloucestershire and Martin Young was batting; Ray Illingworth was bowling and Close was right in there at forward short leg.

For once, Ray bowled a bit of a short ball outside the off stump, which Martin Young pulled and he got Close above his right eye. The ball ballooned up over Jimmy Binks, the wicketkeeper, and into the hands of Phil Sharpe at first slip – caught!

Blood was pouring down Close's face. It didn't worry him, he just wiped it away, and fielded for about another ten minutes. Then the lunch interval came and he walked back – blood still pouring down – and as he went in, one of the members said, 'Mr Close, you mustn't stand as near as that. It's very dangerous. What would have happened if it had hit you slap between the eyes?'

He said, 'He'd have been caught at cover!'

Henry Blofeld:

I would have paid any money in the world to see W.G. Grace. He was obviously a bit of a crook, but he must have been a fine cricketer. There are lots of lovely stories about him, but the one I like most of all is when Neville

Cardus was talking to one of the old Gloucestershire professionals who'd played with W.G. and he asked him, 'Do you think that W.G. ever cheated?'

This old Gloucestershire professional looked at Neville Cardus and said, 'The Old Man cheat? Why, 'e were much too clever for that!'

The other one I like is when he was bowled and the ball just flicked his off bail. The Doctor leant down, picked up the bail and put it back on the stumps, and said, 'Windy day, umpire, isn't it?'

The umpire said, 'Yes it is, Dr Grace, and mind it don't blow your hat off on the way back to the pavilion!'

Dickie Bird:

W.G. Grace was so feared by the umpires of his day that some hardly dared to give him out, and he bent the rules quite unashamedly on more than one occasion. During one innings in a county match he lofted the ball skywards into the outfield, ran one, and, as he turned for the second, noticed a fielder nicely positioned for the catch. He immediately declared the innings – with the ball still in the air – to avoid being given out and having his average spoiled. He claimed that the catch had been taken after close of play!

Henry Blofeld:

There are plenty of stories about W.G. Grace, usually constructed around his inbuilt reluctance to leave the crease when the umpire had indicated otherwise. When he ticked off umpires for giving him out, saying, 'They've come to see me bat, not you umpire,' he was right. He was an institution and the huge crowds came hoping they would see him add to his mountain of runs.

His career as a doctor inevitably came second, but he was still much loved by his patients as he went about his business in a brisk, jovial and efficient way. After a difficult maternity case, he is said to have told his friends, 'Well, the baby's dead and I don't think there's much hope for the mother, but I do believe I shall pull the father through.'

On another occasion, when instructing a mother to put her children, both of whom had high temperatures, to bed, he said, 'There's no need to call me unless they get up to 210 for 2 before lunch!'

David Lloyd:

Jack Simmons was twenty-seven, and a qualified draughtsman with Lancashire County Council, before he came full-time into county cricket, but it's fair to say he made up for lost time. He went on to chair the Lancashire committee, and the club, plainly, is his life. The stories of his eating habits are legion. They are also all true.

I took him home once after a day's play and he asked to be dropped at a chippy, called Jack's, 500 yards from his home. Once he'd bought his fish and chips, he sat down on the wall outside to eat them. It was raining, he lived a block or so away and I was still there waiting to chauffeur him, so I asked what seemed the natural question. 'Why don't you take them home, Jack, eat them in your own kitchen?'

He looked alarmed. He said, 'If I take these home, Jackie'll not make me any supper!'

Fred Trueman:

Charlie Harris once dived to take a catch off Harold Butler and rolled around the ground in agony, claiming he had broken a bone. It was, in fact, nothing more than a dislocation – painful enough, I suppose – and Charlie was taken to hospital for a precautionary X-ray.

When told it was a minor injury and that the dislocation was to be put back into position, he enquired, nervously, 'Will it hurt?'

'Not much,' he was told, and the sleeve was rolled up ready for the simple operation. Charlie took a towel, rolled it up tightly and clenched it between his teeth as the collarbone was put back – and he screamed!

A senior nurse, who was, as it happened, an ardent Notts supporter, reproached him severely. 'There's a nineteen-year-old girl just down the corridor who gave birth to twins this morning,' she told him, 'and she didn't make half so much noise as you.'

'Aye,' replied Charlie, 'but just you try putting 'em back!'

Henry Blofeld:

There may never be a more humorous cricketer than Patsy Hendren. Patsy was a natural clown and wherever he played, he brought joy and happiness to the crowds and to all but the most curmudgeonly of those with or against whom he played.

What enabled Hendren to play the measured fool as he did was his brilliant batting. Only two others, Sir Jack Hobbs and Frank Woolley, have scored more first-class runs than Hendren, and Hobbs is the only one who has scored more than his 170 centuries.

When he was fielding on the boundary he developed

the habit, which always got him a laugh, of chasing a ball in the outfield and bending down as if to pick it up when he was still ten yards short of it. It was no surprise if the batsman fell for it and refused a safe third run.

Hendren loved practical jokes. He tried one at the end of his career on his Middlesex captain, Walter Robins. When Robins was batting, he used to charge down the wicket to the spinners and if he missed the ball he would carry on walking towards the pavilion without a backward glance. Once when Hendren was the non-striker, Robins rushed out of his ground to a spinner, missed and was about to continue to walk when Hendren yelled, 'Look out, he's missed it!'

Robins spun round and threw himself headlong on a muddy pitch to get his bat into his crease. The crowd roared and Robins got up, brushed himself down and then saw that the wicket was broken and the keeper, Harry Elliott, was grinning broadly and tossing the ball from hand to hand!

David Lloyd:

When Lancashire were playing at Blackpool one year, Jack Simmons booked a table in the local fish restaurant. The curious thing was that he didn't book it for dinner but for lunch – on a playing day. I've seldom seen him move so fast as when the bails were lifted for the interval – he was away in his car, with a couple of other players in tow, and I'm told he demolished two specials, pudding, chips and peas with fish on top, and still got back for the first ball of the afternoon.

Occasionally, he didn't even make it. Southport always put on home-made gooseberry and cherry pies for pudding at lunchtime and when the bell went for us to take the field one day, he'd just started on a full one. For an over, Lancashire fielded with ten men. Then Jack emerged from the tent, licking his lips, the cat that got the cream.

He'd often stand at slip with a biscuit in his top pocket, just to keep him going, and he once justified eating two huge apple pies by saying, 'They said I was to eat a lot of fruit!'

Unsurprisingly, Jack Simmons was a very poor pre-season trainer, especially when it came to the five-mile run that would often complete our session in those days. He was once spotted climbing down from a lorry at the gates of Old Trafford, having tailed himself off from the rest of us and convinced the driver he was lost!

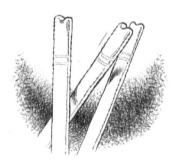

Brian Johnston:

On one occasion Patsy Hendren was fielding on the boundary by the famous Hill on the Sydney Cricket Ground. The batsman hit the ball high in the air towards him. As it soared higher and higher into the air a raucous voice from the Hill shouted, 'Patsy, if you miss the catch, you can sleep with my sister.'

Later Patsy was asked what he had done. 'Oh,' he replied, 'as I hadn't seen his sister, I caught the ball!'

Graeme Fowler:

Steve O'Shaughnessy, the Lancashire all-rounder, is very talented. But he speaks before he thinks, and often acts before he has worked out what he is doing. That can be very funny – he is a master of spoonerisms and *non sequiturs*. For instance, a woman came into a pub where we were. She had obviously just come back from Majorca or wherever, since she had this beautiful, deep tan, and Shauny asked her, 'Are you a sunship worper?'

On the same day a kid asked him for his autograph, proferring a cigarette packet. Shauny said, 'Have you no paper? I'm not signing that pag facket!'

Once a girl rang the dressing room for him when he wasn't there. He was given the message – she would ring back later, but didn't leave a name.

'Oh.' Pause. 'Was she a blonde?'

On another occasion he was out playing golf with Pete Lever, and Pete, who is a keen bird-watcher, said, 'Listen, that's a green woodpecker.'

'Oh.' Pause. 'How can you tell it's green?'

Justin Langer:

Of all the finger spinners I encountered, Phil Tufnell had the best shape to his delivery. If he'd had more confidence in himself – like a Warne or a Muralitharan – he could have been one of the great English spinners. Instead, he turned out to be a sometime match-winner and an all-time classic character.

I never played with anyone who doubted himself as much as 'The Cat' did. It made him arguably the toughest bloke I ever had to captain. During the 2000 season at Middlesex, it wasn't unusual for him to ring me two or three times a night, worrying about his performance, worrying he'd let himself down and the team. No matter how many times I told him not to worry, he could never be placated.

He could be impossible on the field as well. One day at Lord's he simply walked off. He didn't say a word, just disappeared, and left us with ten men on the ground. When he finally wandered back, I asked him where he had gone.

'To have a smoke,' he replied, as if surprised at my question.

'You are kidding me.'

I was unsure how to respond, or what to do, and Tuffers wasn't waiting around to find out. He turned and began heading down to fine leg, calling out over his shoulder, 'Aww, the stress, skipper, the stress!'

Graeme Fowler:

In September 1985 I went to the Lancashire end-of-season party. I had been out of the first team for a few weeks because of a neck injury, so I didn't really fancy it at all – but it was great fun. Everyone was presented with a memento. I was given my second-team cap and an electric switch so that I could switch myself back on. Andy Hayhurst, known as 'Anus', got one of those big plastic tie-on bottoms that you strap round your waist – predictable but quite funny. David Hughes, who was moving into insurance as an outside interest, was given a bowler hat and a false nose – he has a large natural one.

Chris Maynard was given a dustbin lid with empty cans of lager tied round it – they reckoned he drank too much and they called him Grover after the character in *Sesame Street*, because he was always moaning and never had a good word to say about anybody. The hat was quite effective – it looked like an Australian hat, so he had it on all night.

Steve O'Shaughnessy was given a goldfish in a goldfish bowl. He was told, 'The reason we've given you this, Shauny, is we want you to watch it all winter. You'll see that no matter how many times it opens its mouth, nothing comes out.' John Stanworth then stuffed Shauny out of sight. He stuck his hand in the bag with the goldfish in the bowl, got this bit of carrot out, waggled it around and then ate it. Shauny went mad. 'You've eaten me fish! You've eaten me fish! The rotten git, he's eaten me fish!'

Of course everybody fell about. But then to cap it all, at the end of the evening just as everyone was leaving, Shauny was in the foyer carrying his fish and this drunken Scot rolled up to him, picked the fish out of the bowl and *did* eat it. This time Shauny thought, 'Oh, it's another bit of carrot, I'm not falling for that one again.' But in fact the Scotsman had quite calmly picked the fish out of the bowl, eaten it, and then cleared off as if nothing had happened.

Shauny was left with a bowl of water!

Michael Parkinson:

When David Lloyd decided to play cricket for a living, the Wheel Tappers and Shunters Club lost a good comic. What cricket gained was a player able enough to captain his county, Lancashire, and almost captain his country.

He had an outside chance to be captain of England in 1980, when he was brought back for the one-day internationals against the West Indies. Lloyd's account of what happened is a perfect example of his droll style.

'I was told I'd be batting number seven and if I showed up well, got a few runs and handled the quicks okay, I would be in with a chance with a couple of others when it came to the captaincy. I remember taking guard and watching Malcolm Marshall walking back to his bowling mark. I thought to myself, I don't go that far on my holidays!

'He set off towards me. He was halfway there when I thought, I bet he doesn't want me to play forward to this delivery. He let go this ninety-miles-per-hour thunderbolt at me and I played what I can only describe as a very hurried backward defensive prod. The ball smashed into my forearm and broke it in two places.

'As I was helped from the field, I remember thinking, I wonder if I've done enough?'

Dickie Bird:

Two of the greatest characters to have left the Test match scene are Ian Botham and Allan Lamb. I was glad when they went, really, because they were always taking the mickey out of me during a Test match. Once I came in from square leg to stand at the bowler's end and Ian

Botham had set off a pile of Chinese firecrackers behind the stumps!

In a Test match at Trent Bridge, England were playing the West Indies. England had lost two wickets very quickly and Allan Lamb came out to bat at number four. He walked down the members' enclosure at Trent Bridge, out on to the middle, and he came towards me at square leg. I thought, 'What's he coming over to me for at square leg?' I said, 'Lamby, we're playing over there!'

He said, 'I want *you*.'

I thought, oh dear, and I asked, 'What do you want, man?'

He said, 'When I padded up and put my gloves on, I rushed to get out at the fall of the wicket and I forgot to take my mobile phone out of my pocket.'

I said, 'What do you want me to do with that?'

He replied, 'I want you to put it in your pocket and if it rings, I want you to answer it.'

'We're in the middle of a Test match, man,' I said. 'You'll get me shot.'

He said, 'Shove it in your pocket and if it rings, I'm expecting some important messages.'

Lamby went off and took guard off my colleague and soon he was playing away. Then after about five overs, the phone started to ring in my pocket.

'Hello?' I said, 'Who's there?'

'This is Ian Botham, ringing from the dressing room.'

'What do you want?' I said. 'I've enough problems out here.'

'Tell that fellow Lamb to play a few shots or get out.'

I said, 'Lamby . . . it's for you!'

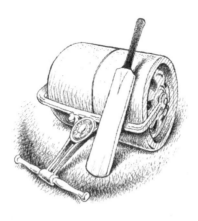

COUNTY CAPERS

Dickie Bird:

If you were to ask cricket lovers to nominate the most beautiful county ground many would go for Worcester, with good reason. You look through the trees to the cathedral and the River Severn, and when the flowers at New Road are in full bloom, it really is a marvellous sight.

Another feature at Worcester is the space reserved in the car park for the tea ladies. One anxious reporter, having arrived late at the ground for an important fixture, was looking for somewhere to park, when the attendant told him, 'Sorry, sir, I'm afraid you can't come in, there are no spaces left.'

'Yes, there are,' replied the reporter, pointing to several vacant spots.

'Oh,' said the attendant, 'but those are reserved for the tea ladies, sir.'

'But you surely don't need all that space for them,' complained the increasingly frustrated hack.

'Oh, but we do, sir,' replied the attendant. 'And I'll tell you this for nothing – it's a lot more important that we get our tea than you get anything in the paper, young man!'

Clive Radley:

A local derby – Middlesex v Surrey at Lord's. Pat Pocock (known throughout cricket as 'Percy') arrived at the crease to bat wearing spectacles, which nobody had seen him wearing before.

Fred Titmus, the bowler, politely inquired, 'What have you got those things on the end of your nose for, Perce?'

'They are because I'm bloody deaf. Why do you think?'

Titmus then bowled Pocock with his first delivery. As the dejected batsman walked past him back to the pavilion, Titmus remarked, 'You didn't hear that one too well, though, did you?'

Brian Johnston:

I am very much in favour of having a drink now and again because I think it is sociable but, in my job, you should never have too much. Of course, the same applies to cricket and I'll give you a good example. It concerns dear old 'Hopper' Levett. W.H.V. Levett was a great wicketkeeper and he kept wicket once for England against India, but mainly he used to keep for Kent when

Les Ames or Godfrey Evans were playing for England. A very good wicketkeeper indeed, he stood up marvellously on the leg side. A great chap. He liked a glass of beer, and he smoked a foul-smelling pipe, but he was a lovely person.

One night, in 1947, he did have rather a heavy night and the next morning he had a most ghastly hangover. He went into the Kent dressing room and they helped him on with his socks and his boots, his pads, his box and his shirt. Kent were fielding, so they pushed him out on to the field, and a young fast bowler called Harding – who sadly died shortly after – had the ball.

So they put Levett down eighteen yards behind the stumps. He got down – he couldn't get any lower, his head was throbbing – and the first ball went *pheeww* past his right ear. He hadn't moved. Four byes. The next one went *pheeww* past his left ear. Four byes. That's eight byes in two balls and he hadn't moved.

The third ball, though, was outside the leg stump and the batsman reached forward and got an outside edge. The ball went very low on the leg side and old 'Hopper' took off and held a most brilliant catch, inches from the ground.

He threw the ball up in the air, went across to the slips and said, 'Do you know, gentlemen, I think that's the first time I've ever caught a batsman off the first ball of the day!'

Dickie Bird:

Yorkshire still play the odd game at Scarborough, a super ground, and their visits attract big gates. Scarborough is well known for the cricket festival, when various trophies are played for by Yorkshire and visiting guest teams. The cliffs overlooking the glorious North Bay are close at hand on one side of the ground, although not visible to the spectators, but there is a marvellous view of the North Yorkshire moors on the opposite side.

Bill Bowes, one of the best bowlers Yorkshire and England have ever had, covered cricket for the *Yorkshire Evening Post* when he retired from playing. He was faced with the usual problems of telephoning his reports from the ground to the sports desk back in Leeds, and during one Scarborough Festival week he sent the following item, 'After a quiet spell, Parfitt went down the wicket to Illingworth and edged him over the slips and into the deep for three.'

Unfortunately, the young lady on copy-taking duty that day had no interest whatsoever in cricket, and she typed out, 'After a quiet spell, Parfitt went down the wicket to Illingworth and edged him over the cliffs and into the deepest parts of the sea!'

Keith Fletcher:

It was in the early days of sponsorship, and Essex were due to play Middlesex the next day. We arrived at Lord's to find a large notice in the dressing room saying: 'NO TRACKSUITS ALLOWED ON THE PLAYING AREA'.

The Essex players, wearing our first sponsored tracksuits, had wandered down on to the hallowed turf to start fielding practice. Colonel John Stephenson, then secretary of MCC (a delightful man) saw us from his office window and announced over the Tannoy, 'No tracksuits to be worn on the playing area. Please remove your tracksuits!'

We all dutifully removed the offending apparel to reveal cricket whites – everyone, that is, except Ray East, who had nothing on *at all* under his tracksuit.

The Colonel, still on the Tannoy and in his best Oxford accent, said, 'Sensibly!'

Brian Johnston:

The famous umpire Bill Reeves was seldom at a loss for a reply. But even he was struck dumb when Surrey were playing Gloucestershire at Cheltenham and Alf Gover, Surrey's traditional number eleven, strode to the crease. Gover took up his stance ready to withstand the onslaught, scorning to take guard. Noting this somewhat irregular behaviour, Reeves said, 'Hey, Alf, don't you want your guard?'

'No, thanks,' said Alf, 'I've played here before!'

Martin Johnson:

Leicestershire, so the match scorer alleges, beat York-shire by nine runs at Scarborough on 31 August 1979 to win the Fenner Trophy. We'll have to take his word for it, as close on 7000 people barely witnessed a ball bowled in the most remarkable cricket match I've ever seen, or to be precise, never seen.

In the best 'show must go on' tradition, the big holi-day crowd basked in a fog so thick it would have grounded every aircraft in the country. Only the occa-sional thwack of leather on willow convinced them that, somewhere in the vicinity, a cricket match was taking place – and this was in a year when the sponsors ordered the band to keep quiet during play to add a note of seriousness to the proceedings. I preferred the suggestion that they should strike up with, say, 'Colonel Bogey' when someone was out for a duck, or perhaps 'Slowboat to Australia' if Boycott had been batting. At least then we would have had a vague idea what was going on.

No soccer match would have started, but this game

got under way just forty minutes late. It would have been thirty-five had the umpires not forgotten to bring out the ball. Leicestershire made a fine start thanks to Briers, who cracked six fours in his 36. I can only assume his breakfast consisted of carrot juice. Yorkshire opened with Old and Stevenson. For obvious reasons I can't tell you whether they performed well, although the bowling analyses indicate that Stevenson probably did not.

Mind you, analyses might not be much to go by. During the later part of the innings, the ball crossed the ropes in front of the press box with not a player in sight. The scorer took a guess and gave it to Clift off Stevenson, although it could just as easily have been to Birkenshaw off Oldham.

Dudleston's 14 in 21 overs suggested that he's happier batting when he can see the ball, but Davison and Balderstone put together a useful stand of 50 in only 11 overs before both fell in successive deliveries. Clift and Birkenshaw did even better, putting on 70 crucial runs in the last 11 overs. Birkenshaw's blade seemed to send the ball across the boundary every time it was wielded. But, once again, one could only get a vague impression of events. A tremendous cheer went up while these two were batting. Was it a six or was someone out? Then, as the mist lifted for a second or two, we noticed a beer lorry trundling through the main gates.

Leicestershire seemed destined to enjoy their ale more than their opponents would halfway through the Yorkshire innings when they stood at 79 for 3, still needing another 147. Shuttleworth then came on without anyone knowing it and removed Sharp, apparently lbw, and Sidebottom, appropriately enough, caught behind. Old, however, possesses a bat like a railway sleeper and, with sixes off Clift and Shuttleworth and a stand of 31 in three overs with Cope, he brought the target down from 46 off five overs to 10 off the last five balls. Higgs dropped short, Old hooked high and Briers took a well-judged catch to end it.

Simon Hughes:

On Sundays at Lord's during my benefit year at Middlesex in 1991, I took the unprecedented step of persuading several young women to go round with the buckets instead of the loyal old supporters who normally did it, and they regularly brought in £1000 plus. The English currency – mostly coins but sometimes the odd fiver – was always augmented by francs, dollars, fruit-machine tokens and any other shrapnel people happened to have in their pockets.

It was the usual practice for the MCC to broadcast the proceeds over the Tannoy once they had been counted, and one Sunday I got them to announce: 'Simon

Hughes thanks everyone who donated to today's benefit collection, which raised one thousand two hundred and thirty pounds, thirty pence, seventy Canadian cents, fifty pesetas, one Kenyan shilling and two Iranian shekels.'

It got a better response than anything I'd ever achieved on the field, and all the collectors chuckled with self-satisfaction. We weren't quite so amused when the next morning we read that Bryan Robson's benefit match at Old Trafford had raised £340,000!

Dickie Bird:

Cedric Rhodes used to be the chairman of Lancashire County Cricket Club and one day he asked Farokh Engineer, in view of the continued hostilities between India and Pakistan, if there was any likelihood that he would be going home to fight for his country.

'Only if the fighting reaches my village,' said Farokh. 'Then, of course, I will have to go to protect my wife and children.'

Rhodes enquired, 'Which village is that?'

And Farokh replied, 'Altrincham!'

Richard Whiteley:

During the Scarborough Festival an avid young Yorkshire fan comes upon a stall at the local fairground announcing 'Marvo, the Miracle Memory Man'.

Intrigued, the fan enters the tent and finds, to his surprise, a Native American Indian lounging in a chair and drawing very slowly on his pipe.

'All right, mate?' says the Yorkshireman. The Indian removes the pipe from his mouth and with steely eyes says quietly, 'Where I come from, it is customary to greet a stranger with the word "How".'

Feeling a little intimidated, the fan responds, 'How, Marvo, what is this all about then?'

'I have a perfect and infallible memory,' says Marvo. 'Ask me anything.'

I'll get this bugger, says the fan to himself and asks, 'Who won the Gillette Cup final in 1965?'

'Yorkshire beat Surrey by 175 runs, 4 September 1965.'

'That's amazing,' says the Yorkshireman, and leaves shortly afterwards.

Some fifteen years later, the now-seasoned fan is back at the Festival and is most surprised to come upon Marvo, the Native American memory man again.

'How,' he greets him.

Replies Marvo, 'Boycott 146, Illingworth 5 for 29.'

Brian Johnston:

Arthur Wood, the Yorkshire wicketkeeper, was in a match with a batsman who had played at and missed three successive balls, each of which just grazed the stumps without disturbing the bails. Arthur asked him, 'Have you ever tried walking on water?'

On another occasion Yorkshire were playing the South Africans at Bramall Lane in 1935 and H.B. Cameron went in to face the bowling of Hedley Verity. Cameron took guard and hit the first ball over the pavilion for six. The next three balls all went for four and the last two for six each, making 30 runs off the over.

When Verity passed Arthur Wood at the end of the over, his face was as long as a collie's.

'Don't you worry, Hedley,' said Wood, 'you've got him in two minds.'

'Two minds?' said Verity. 'What do you mean, two minds?'

'Oh,' said Wood, 'he doesn't know whether to hit you for four or six!'

Vic Marks:

In 1983 a few cracks were appearing at Somerset and changes were in the air. Derek Taylor, our trusty wicket-keeper, had retired. Taylor was replaced behind the stumps by Trevor Gard, who came from South Petherton in south Somerset. He was no more than five feet five inches tall and he had wonderful hands, though his lack of inches could sometimes make keeping to Joel Garner a trial. He was – and still is – a delightful West Countryman, who does not like to get too excited about anything. Which is not really what is required from the modern wicketkeeper.

Sometimes his sense of fair play could be infuriating. I once delivered one of my most vociferous lbw appeals, which was rejected. It did not help my cause that Trevor behind the stumps had not joined in the appeal. So at the end of the over, I asked him why.

'Missing by a quarter of an inch!' he said.

Simon Hughes:

I discovered a whole new vocabulary during my opening season in first-class cricket in 1980. Here's a list of the jargon I learned:

Aerosol bowler Someone, usually a paceman, who 'sprays it everywhere'.

Bunsen (burner) Turning pitch. Raging bunsens are often found in India.

Cafeteria bowling A load of dross, so the batsman can 'help himself'.

Cardboard cut-outs Immobile slip fielders.

Crusted Batsman hit on head by a bouncer.

Dinkies Second team.

Dollies Stumps.

Donks Outfielders, usually lumbering fast bowlers.

Filth Bowling that promotes a flier.

Flier Rapid run-scoring at the start of an innings.

German general Batting side encouraging the ball to boundary (after Goebbels).

Gnat Seam bowler of negligible pace.

Grabbers Slip fielders.

Headless chicken Bowler who tears in wildly with a crazed expression.

Jaffa Unplayable delivery.

Jugged, going for the jug Bowler savaged by a rampant batsman.

Knacker Ball, delivery.

Lenny Batsman who favours leg-side shots.

Nick Faint edge, or another word for 'form'.

On 'em Batsman arriving for the second innings having got nought in the first.

Pongo Rapid scoring.

Rabbit Hopeless tailender.

Sawn off Dodgy umpiring decision.

Spitting cobra Delivery that rears abruptly from a length.

Strangle Wicket with rotten delivery. The bowler is often labelled 'Boston'.

Trolleyed Player (usually the captain) losing his temper.

Up the ladder Injured player suspected of hypochondria.

Xs Captain's allowance for a round of drinks after a day's play.

Fred Trueman:

George Hirst was a magnificent player for Yorkshire and England in the early part of the twentieth century and he later became an excellent coach. In one remarkable season George scored 2385 runs and took 208 wickets.

When asked if he thought anyone would ever beat it, he replied, 'I don't know, but if he does he'll be bloody tired!'

Brian Johnston:

In a Lancashire match a fast bowler was bowling on a bad wicket, and the opening batsman had to face a number of terrifying deliveries. The first whizzed past his left ear, the second nearly knocked his cap off, and the third struck him an awful blow over the heart. He collapsed and lay on the ground – then, after a minute or two, he got up and prepared to take strike again. The umpire asked him if he was ready and he replied, 'Yes, but I would like the sightscreen moved.'

'Certainly,' said the umpire. 'Where would you like it?'

The batsman replied, 'About halfway down the wicket between me and the bowler!'

Dickie Bird:

A Yorkshireman who played with Northamptonshire in the 1950s was Des Barrick, a big practical joker, who was born in the same row of terraced houses as Geoff Boycott.

The legendary fast bowler Frank Tyson was one of Des's team-mates. Now Frank did not care much for the ground at Derby, but there was one consolation – the enormous antique baths, ideal for a post-match soak when the old bones were aching like mad and the biting wind had reached the parts that other winds could not reach. One typically freezing day, he had jumped straight in the huge bath and was just beginning to get some feeling back into his fingers and toes when Des 'Roly-Poly' Barrick tiptoed in and poured a bucket of ice-cold water over him.

Frank almost hit the ceiling, not to mention Des. In any case, the cackling Des was off like a shot. So Frank decided on revenge. He wrapped his towel round him, filled another bucket with ice-cold water, marched into the adjoining room where Des was sitting, and poured it over his colleague's head.

Des was fully dressed by this time, and he stood there, as if in a state of shock, with the water soaking into his clothes. A wicked grin slowly spread across his face and Frank was a bit taken aback. Then came the punch-line.

Chortled Des, 'I've got news for thee, Frank, old lad. I rather thought you might try summat like that, so I've put *thy* clothes on!'

Martin Johnson:

Back in 1986, when an opposition batsman sent up a skier at Grace Road, Leicester and the cry from the fielders went up, 'Yours, Ted!', it may not have been immediately apparent to spectators exactly who had been elected to take the catch. They should have kept their eyes on Tim Boon. He, to all in the dressing room, was the aforementioned 'Ted'. He bore no resemblance to a former Conservative Prime Minister, didn't need a fluffy toy to soothe himself to sleep, and was too young to have gone through his teens wearing winklepickers, hair slicked back with Brylcreem. So why Ted?

It dated back to a civic reception in Bristol two years earlier, when the players, all togged up, were being introduced by one of those uniformed commissionaires with a booming toastmaster's voice. 'Name, please,' he inquired. 'Tim Boon,' came the whispered reply. 'Ladies and gentlemen, I present . . . Mr Ted Moon!' Collapse of assembled cricketers. The name stuck, and Boon was instantly lifted out of the category in which 90 per cent of cricketers find themselves when the nicknames are handed out – just add a 'y'. 'Boony, Cobby, Steeley, Baldy, Benjy, Potsy, Aggy . . .'

Nicknames are compulsory for county cricketers. It must be something to do with the boarding-school syndrome, where everyone is away from home and lumped together. For prep school read dressing room, for dormitory read hotel bedroom. When Laurie Potter arrived at Grace Road, David Gower temporarily gave up on the *Telegraph* crossword, and pondered about the new man. 'How about "Lobster"?' Lobster, Potter, get it? Anyway, it didn't stick.

Most nicknames are boring, others unable to be reproduced in a family publication. Some are quite good. Romaines was 'Human', Aworth 'Rita', Derrick 'Bo', Weston 'Spaghetti', Bakker 'Nip', and dear old Graham Parsons, not noted for shrewdness or clarity of vision when the heat was on out in the middle, was 'Cement-head'.

David Steele picked up one of the better ones. His fondness for being last in the queue when the rounds were being bought remains legendary, and so he became 'Crime' – doesn't pay!

GAFFES AND GIGGLES

Christopher Martin-Jenkins:

I have been a cricket commentator for many years and one clever dick once referred to the term 'gross ignorance' as being 144 sports commentators. I thought it was quite clever, but one of my colleagues, who shall be nameless, said, 'That's all very well. But why 144?'

I started from very small beginnings. The first match that the BBC ever let me loose on was between Surrey and Yorkshire towards the end of one season in the early 1970s and it had been a very good morning for Chris Old, then a young Yorkshire all-rounder, and I finished my report at lunchtime for the World Service by saying, 'Above all, it has been a very good morning for young Old.'

To which Paddy Feeny, who was an extremely witty presenter for the BBC World Service, replied, 'Oh, really? I used to know his father, old Young!'

Brian Johnston:

One serious bit of advice. Nothing to do with cricket really, but if you're making a speech at a cricket dinner, or anywhere, and you make a mistake, never stop to apologise, because if you do, people know you've made a mistake. If you don't apologise and go straight on, people say, 'What did he say?' and, by that time, you're talking about something else.

I've carried this out over my cricket career, because I'm famous for making quite a lot of gaffes. I don't do them on purpose, but in a six-hour day you're bound to make the odd mistake. A lot of them are very old, but here are one or two:

In 1961 at Headingley, the Australians were fielding and I was doing the television. The camera panned in and showed Neil Harvey at leg slip, and he filled the screen. Now if you're doing a television commentary and someone fills the screen, you've got to be very quick to talk about him, otherwise the camera goes off and shows something else and you've missed the chance.

So without thinking, very hurriedly, I said, 'There's Neil Harvey standing at leg slip, with his legs wide apart waiting for a tickle!'

I realised immediately what I'd said and wished the earth would open and swallow me up. The Australian commentator Jack Fingleton made matters worse by drawing attention to it, saying, 'I beg your pardon. I presume you mean waiting for a catch.'

I didn't speak for about three minutes after that!

Then I went to Hove, for radio, where Sussex were playing Hampshire. Hampshire had a chap called Henry Horton who had a funny stance. When he batted, he stood more or less parallel to the ground, leaned right forward and stuck his bottom out.

I thought I ought to let the listeners know, so I said, 'He's got a funny stance, he sticks his bottom out.'

Then I meant to say, 'He looks like he's *sitting* on a *shooting* stick,' but I got it the wrong way round!

When Ray Illingworth was captaining Leicestershire, the studio came over to me and I said, 'Welcome to Leicester, where Ray Illingworth has just relieved himself at the Pavilion End!'

And at Worcester I once greeted the listeners with, 'Welcome to Worcester, where you've just missed seeing Barry Richards hitting one of Basil D'Oliveira's balls clean out of the ground!'

David Gower:

There will be times – and many of them – as either a presenter or a commentator, when the words don't come out quite right and all you can do is live with it. I find a smile helps ease the pain both for me and the viewer, though there is always the dilemma whether or not to admit to having mangled the language or having botched the odd word. Richie Benaud, whose advice I always valued supremely, had a simple theory: 'Let the viewer at the other end worry about it.'

Nowadays, in the ever-competitive world of the Sky commentary box, any mispronunciation is likely to be pounced upon by one's fellow commentators, so any chance of 'letting the viewers worry about it' tends to disappear in a nanosecond.

There are times when one just cannot cover up the error. I was in the studio at Lord's with Michael Atherton one lunchtime a summer or two ago and we had a feature on Charlotte Edwards, the very talented and successful captain of the England women's team. It was a great piece, reflecting well on Charlotte, who had just become the most capped female player for England.

I had introduced the piece with all the words in the right order, but my attempt to 'back announce' it as it finished went awry, and I described Charlotte as the most 'fapped' player (some sort of elision between female and capped). Luckily, 'fapped' remains a non-word and utterly meaningless. The trouble is that it does, I admit, sound possibly rude and Athers was chortling loudly no sooner had the word left my mouth.

No chance to recover from that one then!

Brian Johnston:

John Snagge was a marvellous chap. He was the voice of Great Britain. Every big occasion – the Allied landings, Winston Churchill's death, the King's death – he was always the voice they put on the air and he represented us all.

He was a tremendous announcer in that way but he didn't normally do the sports news. One day he was asked to read it and he got as far as the cricket scores, when he said, 'Yorkshire two hundred and fifty-nine all out. Hutton ill . . . Oh, I'm sorry, Hutton one hundred and eleven!'

Dickie Bird:

My most embarrassing moment as an umpire was when nature called and I came off the field at Old Trafford and stopped a Test match. Ian Botham was bowling from my end and I said, 'I've got to go off, Both, I've got to go to the toilet.'

He said, 'You can't, we're in the middle of a Test match. There's still an hour left to go before lunch.'

I said, 'I've got to go,' and he said, 'Well, if you gotta go, you gotta go!'

So I said, 'I'm sorry, gentlemen, but nature calls.'

I just ran off the field, went into the toilet, and came back down the members' enclosure at Old Trafford. It was a full house and as I came out, I was pulling up my zip . . . and the crowd erupted!

Brian Johnston:

I was at Southampton one Saturday to commentate on a match between Hampshire and Surrey. Rex Alston was up at Edgbaston covering one of Warwickshire's matches and close of play there was not until 7 p.m.

At 6.30 p.m. at Southampton, as the players left the field, I said something like, 'Well, that's close of play here with Hampshire three hundred and one all out. But they go on playing till seven o'clock at Edgbaston, so over there now for some more balls from Rex

Alston!'

Rex himself is reputed to have said, 'Over now to Old John Arlott at Trafford!' He also once reported that a captain had asked for 'the medium pace roller!'

Then at Lord's during a Middlesex match, Rex surprised many listeners when he announced, 'No runs from that over bowled by Jack Young, which means that he has now had four maidens on the trot!'

Ian Brayshaw:

Even the legendary Australian radio commentator Alan McGilvray occasionally did not say things quite how he might have meant them to be. Like the time in the heart of the 1980/81 season when he summed up a batting failure by Kim Hughes:

'Well, it has been a weekend of delight and disappointment for Kim Hughes – his wife presented him with twins yesterday . . . and a "duck" today!'

Brian Johnston:

We receive thousands of letters at *Test Match Special*, but the writers don't always understand us. Some of the letters are marvellous and there are two I always keep on file.

Once I said that Freddie Titmus was coming on to

bowl and I added, 'He's got two short legs, one of them square.' A woman wrote in, 'No need to be rude about people's disabilities!'

On another occasion Ken Barrington had made 111 and I said, 'He's batting very well now. He's a bit lucky – he was dropped when two.' In came a letter saying, 'Mothers should be more careful with their babies!'

Fred Trueman:

Johnners once received a letter at *Test Match Special* that even he deemed was inadvisable to read over the airwaves. It came after a streaker had been led away by a policeman who diplomatically placed his helmet over the streaker's most treasured possessions. With an innocence that matched Brian's, the lady correspondent asked, 'Could you please tell us – what was the policeman's hat size?'

Brian Johnston:

My most unfortunate gaffe was in 1969 at Lord's where Alan Ward of Derbyshire was playing in his very first Test match, bowling very fast from the Pavilion End to Glenn Turner of New Zealand.

Off the fifth ball of one of his overs, he got Glenn Turner a terrible blow in the box. Turner collapsed, his bat going one way, his gloves another. The cameras panned in and I had to waffle away, pretending he had been hit anywhere but where he had – as it was a bit rude!

After about three minutes he got up, someone gave him his bat, and I said, 'He looks very pale. Very plucky of him, he's going on batting. One *ball* left!'

On another occasion I was doing a commentary on the annual Whitsun match at Lord's. Middlesex always used to play Sussex, and Middlesex were batting, captained by John Warr. They had made about 300 for 3 by tea and I handed back to the studio for the tea interval. They came back to me after tea with, 'Over now to Brian Johnston for the latest news at Lord's.'

'Well,' I said, 'the latest news at Lord's is that Warr's declared.' And, you've got to believe it, the BBC duty officer said an old lady rang up to see who it was against!

Henry Blofeld:

A big problem we have in the commentary box is the awful one of spoonerisms, which absolutely haunt me. I remember one time at Lord's in the early nineties, when India were playing and Gooch scored 333 and then a hundred in the second innings. I was on the air when he got his three-hundredth run. Ravi Shastri, the left-arm spinner, was bowling and Gooch tickled him round the corner and, of course, there was an absolute crescendo of noise.

I was describing this and I thought I'd stop talking and just let the noise carry on. Then I thought something vaguely Churchillian was required, so metaphorically I put my thumbs in my braces and I said, 'Never before in the history of this great ground of ours have so many runs been scored by one batsman in the same innings in a Test match,' and I got rather a taste for it.

Sadly, I had another go at it and I said, 'Never before in the history of this great ground of ours has a cloud *crapped* like this one!'

Peter Baxter:

Christopher Martin-Jenkins' career was peppered with the odd gaffes. There was a time when *Test Match Special* was in some doubt about its future: would there be a network to carry it? That happened many times in our past.

BBC Radio had just got a new managing director in

charge, a woman called Liz Forgan, who was very good actually, and she wanted to meet the commentary team on her visit to Lord's. So I agreed to take her up to the commentary box and introduced her all round. Unfortunately, Christopher was on the air commentating at that time, and missed out on the introductions. However, he got up, came to the back of the box, and saw this woman standing there. He stood there for a bit, worked out who she was, and said, 'My family think you are awfully good in *Blackadder*.'

She looked slightly mystified and moved away from the lunatic. Christopher muttered to me, 'That *was* Miriam Margolyes, wasn't it?'

Somehow, *Test Match Special* survived.

Barry Johnston:

After the famous 'leg-over' incident in 1991, when Johnners and Jonathan Agnew both collapsed into fits of the giggles while doing an end-of-play summary at The Oval [*see the final chapter*], Brian told Peter Baxter that he thought it was not safe for them to work together on air again. 'I know if we look at each other,' he worried, 'it will be hopeless.'

However, nearly a year later, during the Second Test against Pakistan at Lord's, Baxter felt it was time for the two of them to have another try at doing the summary, although Brian insisted that he sat in the left-hand corner of the commentary box and Aggers sat in the right-hand corner, with their heads turned away so they could not catch each other's eye.

Even this extraordinary tactic failed, when Brian suddenly described Javed Miandad as having played a most unusual stroke by 'opening his legs like a croquet hoop and tickling the ball between them'!

Aggers could not believe his ears and when he glanced over at Brian, he could see that Johnners was already going red in the face, and within seconds they were both helpless with the giggles again. This time, however, Brian had learned his lesson and rather than trying to struggle through the scorecard with high-pitched squeaks and wheezes, he kept quiet, not daring to speak at all. With Aggers also speechless, for the next few moments the only sound was the door of the commentary box being slammed on the way out by a furious Baxter.

The silence went on for so long that Agnew's Aunt Peggy, listening at home, thought that her radio had gone dead and took it apart to replace the batteries!

Henry Blofeld:

I'm often asked, what was your most embarrassing moment? I can answer that without any hesitation whatever. It was a long time ago now, I was working for the *Guardian*, and I was travelling around England at great speed. I went up to Old Trafford for a couple of days, I went to Sheffield for another couple of days, then I went to Trent Bridge, and I stayed at one high-rise hotel after another. When I arrived in Nottingham I was booked into a new hotel that had just opened and I found myself on the ninth floor.

I was watching Nottinghamshire play Gloucestershire, and I'd had a little bit of a drink at Trent Bridge at the end of the day's cricket, so I caught a taxi back to the hotel. I had a bath, which is something I occasionally do, changed and put on a clean shirt and took a book down to dinner. I had an extremely good dinner with a very, very good bottle of wine. I remember it very well and I was rather surprised to find it there. So by the time I got to bed, I was 'very nicely thank-you', I suppose.

My trouble started because, ever since my keepers allowed me to, I have discarded pyjamas and I've always slept in the raw – I found it easier that way. So I got into bed and fell asleep, which was absolutely splendid, but I woke up soon afterwards at about a quarter to two to answer the call of nature.

Well, whereas most of us would flick on the switch at the side of the bed and negotiate our way into the bathroom that way, I thought all these high-rise buildings are exactly the same, the bathroom's in exactly the same place, look, no hands, I'll do it in the dark!

I got out of bed and I turned right and turned left and I found the handle of the door, turned it and went out. To my amazement the light was on, which rather surprised me. Then I looked and saw there was a wall about six feet in front of me. I thought, that's strange, there's no loo at all. Then I heard a great clunk behind me ... you've guessed it, the door of my room had slammed shut and there I was, stark bollock naked on the ninth floor of this hotel in Nottingham.

It's quite a predicament. I really didn't know what to do. I was befuddled with sleep and my sense of judgement was gravely impaired. I wandered aimlessly up and down the corridor hoping for a staircase, but I couldn't find one. There was a lift, but I was rather apprehensive of the lift. Suddenly I saw, in a little nook outside a door, a tea tray; there was a pot on it and underneath the cup was a paper doily, folded into quarters.

I opened it out and held it in front of me and, without trying to show off in any way, it just about did duty. Really, in circumstances like that, there's not very much else one can do. I thought, it's nearly two o'clock in the morning; the night porter might get the thrill of a lifetime but he's a man, it should be all right. So I summoned the lift, which came up and I got into it. There were nine bedroom floors, I was on the top one, then it had buttons with the letters REST for the restaurant, BAR for the bar, and REC for reception.

With great care and precision, because my life depended upon it, I pressed the bottom button with REC on it. That was fine. The lift doors shut and we went down the first nine floors. Then quite suddenly the lift stopped. I thought this was rather strange. I looked up at the lights and it wasn't REC, it was REST.

I stood there shivering and the lift doors opened and to my horror, positively surging towards me, I saw eight ladies in long dresses and eight men in dinner jackets. And there I was! People thought it was terribly funny and came running to have a look – they were almost charging fifty pence a time – until eventually a funny little man came up and said, 'You look in a spot of bother!'

I said, 'How very swift of you to spot it.' Then I told him, 'The man I'm really after is the night porter,' and I realised as soon as I'd said it that I could have rephrased it to advantage.

He said, 'The night porter's over there. I'll go and get him. Keep the lift door open.' Well, that was a button at the top, so I had to do a very delicate operation, with one hand up pressing the button and the other one holding the doily, and to everyone's immense disappointment, I got it more or less right.

Then the night porter came and he thought I was a very suspicious character, but because I'd pressed the bottom button for reception, we went down together in the lift. People were running from floor to floor, so we had the whole thing again at the bar floor, and then at the bottom. Eventually, I got back to my room and the relief was tremendous.

The next morning I went to see the manager of the hotel to apologise, a chap called David Waite, I think his name was. I went into his office and said how sorry I was and he said he had heard what had happened. He said he wanted to ask me one particular question which rather puzzled him.

He said, 'I wondered why you held your doily where you did. You know, most people are recognisable by their faces!'

Brian Johnston:

Finally, there was the gaffe that I didn't know I'd said. I'm still not sure whether I did or not! That was after the 1976 match against the West Indies at The Oval, when I received a letter from a lady called Miss Mainpiece, who wrote:

'Dear Mr Johnston, we do enjoy your commentaries, but you must be more careful, as we have a lot of young people listening. Do you realise what you said the other day? They came over to you as Michael Holding was bowling to Peter Willey and you said, "Welcome to The Oval where the bowler's Holding, the batsman's Willey!"'

UMPIRES

Fred Trueman:

I have known a lot of good umpires and some who were *very* good. I have also encountered a few who don't come into either category. Rarely, though, have I encountered an umpire who wasn't, one way or another, a character.

Alec Skelding was a medium-fast bowler for Leicestershire from 1912 to 1929 and then an umpire for twenty-seven years. He did not retire until he was seventy-two and was still giving a smile to players in his last year.

His humour had a laconic, almost sly quality. I was talking to him once at Northampton just after I had made my first hundred, when he mentioned, 'I once got a hundred, you know.'

Surprised, because Alec's first-class average when he retired was 6.76, I replied, 'Did you really?'

'Aye,' said he. 'I started in April and I finished in September. But I did make a hundred runs!'

Brian Johnston:

Umpires are often treated very badly and I'll give you an example. It concerns Gilbert Harding. Many older people may remember Gilbert Harding on the television programme *What's My Line* – crusty, a brilliant brain, but very intolerant of other people's ignorance. He was a bit rude to them, but he used to send them flowers the next day!

When he was at Ampleforth School he was very short-sighted and very fat, so his headmaster said, 'All right, Harding, you can go for walks instead of playing cricket.'

Now this infuriated the young master, just down from Oxford, who took the cricket. He thought he would get his own back, which is always dangerous, and when he put the teams up on the board for the Masters against the Boys, underneath he put: Umpire – Gilbert Harding.

So Gilbert had to go and umpire and he was not too pleased about it at all. The master went in and hit the boys all around the field. He was 98 not out when a boy, bowling from Gilbert's end, hit him high in the chest and stifled an appeal for leg before wicket. But not before Gilbert had said, 'Out!'

This infuriated the young master who, as he went past Gilbert, said, 'Harding! I wasn't out! You weren't paying attention.'

Gilbert thought for a moment and said, 'On the contrary, sir. I *was* paying attention, and you weren't out!'

Alastair Cook:

Graeme Smith assumed the captaincy of South Africa early in his career, at the age of twenty-two, and played with edge and acceptable arrogance until his retirement in 2014. He failed to walk in January 2010 when Ryan Sidebottom claimed for caught behind, following Smith's huge drive in the Fourth Test at the Wanderers stadium, in Johannesburg. There was an obvious noise; if that happens when the batsman is playing well away from his body, he has almost certainly hit it.

On-field umpire Tony Hill disagreed. Since we were playing without the Hot Spot technical aid, and operating an early version of DRS, the England captain Andrew Strauss immediately referred it to Daryl Harper, the third umpire, who upheld the decision. Smith, unbeaten on 15, went on to make 105. South Africa won the match by an innings and squared the series. We were convinced Harper's monitor hadn't had the sound turned on.

When we flew home the following evening, the British Airways pilot, a member of the Barmy Army, woke us as we were preparing for descent into London. After the usual preamble, hoping we had enjoyed the overnight flight, he added, 'You'll be pleased to know that Daryl Harper's ejector seat worked perfectly over the equator!'

Christopher Martin-Jenkins:

A country where touring is toughest and therefore the most fun on the rare occasions when England do win, is, of course, Australia. It used to be even tougher, mind you, in the days when there were no neutral umpires. Many years ago an Aussie passed a graveyard and he noticed the inscription on a grave, which read, 'Here lies an honest man and an umpire.'

He said, 'I see they are burying them two to a grave these days!'

Brian Johnston:

I always like the original umpire story of village cricket, where the home umpire, as they were always called, was umpiring against the visiting side. Their best batsman was hit somewhere high up on the chest, there was an appeal for lbw and the local umpire gave 'out' to the home side.

As he went past, this distinguished-looking batsman said, 'I wasn't out, umpire.'

The umpire gave the traditional reply, 'Well, you look in Wednesday's *Gazette* and see.'

This chap said, '*You* look. I'm the editor!'

Henry Blofeld:

One of the great characters in my years in cricket was Bernard, the late Duke of Norfolk. His family have that wonderful cricket ground at Arundel, in West Sussex, where touring sides often play their first match. It is an absolutely glorious ground and he was a splendid man. He managed the 1962/63 England side in Australia when Ted Dexter was captain.

I was lucky enough to play at Arundel for the Eton Ramblers on a number of occasions and play usually began shortly after 12 o'clock, because the ducal family always went to the Roman Catholic cathedral in Arundel and did a bit of business on their knees before they came along. So it was about ten past twelve before the serious business was likely to be conducted.

Well, on this day, suddenly, up the hill in his Land Rover with the dogs barking in the back, came His Grace the Duke of Norfolk. But when the Duke arrived, there was only one umpire – the other umpire was late.

The Duke said, 'Don't worry, I'll go and get Meadows.'

Now Meadows was his butler, who did duty as umpire occasionally. So the Duke got into his Land Rover with the dogs in the back, drove back down the hill to the castle and went into the butler's pantry, where Meadows was pensively polishing the silver and probably having a second glass of port of the morning. He said, 'Meadows, you must come and umpire.'

So Meadows said, 'Very good, Your Grace,' and got his white coat. He got into the back of the Land Rover with the dogs, because he knew his place, and they went tootling back up the hill.

Well, His Grace the Duke of Norfolk got there in time. Meadows went out to umpire and the Duke rushed out to toss the coin, except he never rushed anywhere. It was always said by P.G. Wodehouse that Beech, who was the butler at Blandings, when he brought the tea out on the lawns in the afternoon, moved 'like a procession of one'. His Grace the Duke of Norfolk moved like a procession of one, I can assure you.

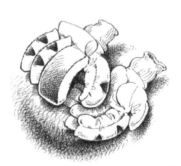

Anyway, his side won the toss and they batted and everything went perfectly swimmingly until quite late in the afternoon when they were about 240 for 7 and the eighth wicket fell. Now His Grace liked to bat. He didn't like the indignity of going in at number eleven, so he put himself in at number ten, where he was grossly over-placed.

The eighth wicket went down and there was a tremendous pause and then this very portly figure with an I Zingari waistcoat – not a jersey but a waistcoat – came out, his tummy leading the procession, and he found himself at the non-striker's end. Now His Grace loved not only to bat but to get off the mark and it was very important, if you wanted to be asked back as the visiting side the following year, that you allowed him to get off the mark. Sometimes it was not at all easy. I remember once, when I was keeping wicket, letting some byes through down the leg side. They went through for a very stately single and the umpire didn't signal the bye and His Grace ruined it all by saying, 'I didn't hit it umpire, it was a bye.' So we had to start all over again.

Well, this time His Grace found himself at the non-striker's end and the chap at the striker's end was quite a decent cricketer, a young subaltern in some regiment. He was playing with His Grace for the first time and he didn't quite know what the form was. He was very, very keen and he played forward to the next ball. He hit it quite firmly to cover point's right hand and said, 'Yes! One!' and set off like a bat out of hell to the other end.

His Grace hadn't got the benefit of synchromesh and getting from a standing start into first gear meant an awful lot of crunching going on. Eventually, he got into first gear and he was just about going at the double, frantically trying to get into second, when the ball came thudding back into the wicketkeeper's gloves from cover point and the bails were taken off with a tremendous appeal.

Meadows was at square leg and the Duke was nowhere to be seen. Meadows had a desperate moment. He thought, my goodness, my job, my pension, the family holiday . . . he saw the whole thing going up in smoke. He didn't know what to do and there was the Duke, puffing like a grampus in the other half of the pitch.

Eventually, Meadows drew himself up to his full height and, to no one in particular at square leg, he said, 'His Grace is not in!'

Brian Johnston:

I support umpires more than 100 per cent, if one can do such a thing. I think they have got a very difficult task and they do a marvellous job. But nowadays they are handicapped by the action replay, which makes their job absolutely impossible.

Umpires have to give a special hand signal if they want the third umpire to look at a replay on television. But soon after this was introduced, Dickie Bird gave the hand signal and the umpire in the pavilion called him up to say, 'Sorry, I was watching *Neighbours!*'

Michael Atherton:

Dickie Bird was a popular but notoriously nervous umpire. Rain and bad weather seemed to follow him as inevitably as night follows day. During a Test match at Old Trafford in 1995, he astonished the natives by bringing off the players because the light was too bright! (It was reflecting off a greenhouse on the practice ground.)

Earlier in that match he interrupted play when he dropped the marbles that he used to count the number of deliveries that had been bowled. Play was halted momentarily while Dickie scrambled around on his hands and knees looking for his counters.

'I've lost me marbles! I've lost me marbles!' he cried.

Most of us thought he had lost his marbles a long time ago.

Brian Johnston:

When I was in Australia with Peter May's team, there was an umpire who wasn't very good. His name was McInnes and on the previous tour with Len Hutton he'd been very good indeed, but somehow he had failed. He made one or two bad mistakes.

Tom Crawford, who used to captain Kent second XI and was a great friend of mine, was talking to Don Bradman about this.

'The trouble with your umpires, Don,' he said, 'is that they've never actually played Test cricket or even Shield cricket. They're not first-class cricketers. They've learnt all the laws and passed exams, but they don't know what goes on in the middle. At home, all our umpires are either Test players or County players.' (That was true then, but I think we've got some now who aren't.)

Don got very indignant about this. 'No, no,' he said. 'What about McInnes? He played for South Australia until his eyesight went.'

Then he realised what he'd said!

Dickie Bird:

They always blame me for bad light, don't they? It's always, 'That Dickie Bird!' They don't realise there's another umpire with me. I remember in a Test match at Old Trafford, Australia were batting and England were fielding. We all came off the field, all the players and the two umpires and we were walking up the members' enclosure to the dressing rooms.

There was a Lancashire member at the top of the members' enclosure, and he'd had so much to drink, he couldn't stand. He said, 'You're 'ere again, Bird, you're 'ere again. Every time you come to Old Trafford, you're always bringing 'em off. Surely it's not bad light? The sun's shining.'

I said, 'No, sir, it's lunchtime!'

Brian Johnston:

There's a dreadful story that dear old Jim Laker used to tell about the Commonwealth tour in India in the 1950s, under Richie Benaud. There was himself, Bruce Dooland and George Tribe of Northants, an Australian, who bowled the chinaman – the left arm off-break.

George was getting the batsmen, time and time again, right up against the stumps, palpably out.

'Howzat!'

'Very close, Mr Tribe.'

'Howzat!!'

'Another inch and I'd have had to raise the finger, Mr Tribe.'

'Howzat!!!'

'Nearly, I had to give him the benefit of the doubt, Mr Tribe. Very difficult.'

George was getting fed up with this and off the sixth ball he more or less yorked the chap, who was right in front of his stumps. It *must* have hit the stumps and he turned round and said, 'What about that?'

The man began, 'Mr . . .' and he got no further than that. George turned round, took him by the throat and said, 'Have another look!'

He said, 'You're right, Mr Tribe. He's out!'

David Lloyd:

The first game I stood in as a first-class umpire was at Fenners in April 1985 and the visitors were Essex. This was the Essex side of the early 1980s who carried all before them and existed on an exhausting diet of pranks and parties. It included characters such as Ray East, Keith Pont and John 'JK' Lever, a superb left-arm bowler who just enjoyed life to the full.

JK opened the bowling from my end when Essex took the field against Cambridge University and his first ball was a slow half-volley. Something not quite right, I thought, but exactly what did not register until the 'ball' struck the bat and disintegrated! Lever had bowled an orange.

Different players needed treating in different ways. With Ian Botham, the sensible umpire would cajole and indulge, without quite letting him run the game. I was standing in a Sunday League match at Taunton when Ian was batting against Wayne Daniel, Middlesex's West Indian fast bowler. It was a televised game and Both was milking the drama of a good finish.

We were midway through the last over and Somerset still required 12 to win. It seemed a long shot but Botham relished those and, as Daniel turned at the end of his run-up, he stood up from his stance and strolled halfway down the pitch, giving it a prod and calling out to me, 'Who are you backing?'

Only Botham could do this but I needed to keep the game moving. 'Three to go and twelve to win is a good contest,' I replied. 'Now, is there any chance of getting on with it, because *Songs of Praise* is next on and we're running late!'

Botham hit two sixes and Somerset won the game!

Brian Johnston:

Charlie Knott of Hampshire was bowling to Dusty Rhodes of Derbyshire and roared out a terrific appeal for a catch at the wicket: 'Howizee?'

To which Alec Skelding replied, 'Oh, he's not at all well and he was even worse last night!'

After another appeal for a run-out, which was a very close thing, Skelding declared, 'Gentlemen, it's a photo finish – and I haven't got time to develop the photo. Not out!'

During another match Johnny Wardle, the Yorkshire and England left-arm spin bowler, inquired of an umpire, 'You know, I think that ball would have hit the wicket. Where do you think it would have hit?'

'How should I know?' retorted the umpire. 'The gentleman's leg was in the way!'

Michael Atherton:

The Second Test against India at Lord's in 1996 was Dickie Bird's farewell match. On the first morning, I organised both teams to line up and applaud him on to the playing surface, and afterwards Alec Stewart and I followed the Indian team out. Bird was in tears. He hugged Mohammad Azharuddin, waved his hankie to all four corners of the ground and thanked me profusely. 'Eh lad, what an honour. I'm so grateful, Mike.'

Srinath bowled the first over of the match to me from Bird's end. He jagged the fifth ball down the Lord's slope and I shuffled across my crease and was trapped in front. Dickie's eyes were still red and he had scarcely wiped the tears from his cheeks, but he rightly waved his forefinger high above his head and shouted, practically bellowed, 'That's aht!'

Brian Johnston:

Surrey were playing Middlesex at The Oval and Bill Reeves was one of the umpires. Nigel Haig opened the bowling and Andrew Sandham went in first for Surrey. Sandham was not very tall and a ball from Haig hit him in the navel. There was a loud appeal.

'Not out,' said Reeves.

'Why not?' asked Haig.

'Too high,' said Reeves.

Haig went back to his mark muttering, possibly thinking that even if a ball hit a little chap like Sandham on the head, it couldn't be too high. A few deliveries later, a beautiful ball beat the batsman all ends up and hit Sandham on the pads.

'What about that one then?' yelled Haig.

'Not out,' said Reeves.

'Why not?' said Haig.

'Too low!' said Reeves . . . and that ended all arguments for that day!

Fred Trueman:

One of the great umpiring remarks of all time must be that of Arthur Jepson, formerly of Notts, who was standing at Old Trafford during that celebrated limited-overs match against Gloucestershire, which went on until a few seconds before 9 p.m.

It was late in the day when Jackie Bond, the Lancashire captain, came in to bat. The lights were on in the pavilion and in Warwick Road station; the moon and stars were clearly visible in the night sky. Bond looked at Jepson and asked, 'What are we doing, playing in this light?'

Jepson replied, tartly, 'What about the light?'

'Well, it's pretty dark, isn't it?' retorted Jackie, staunchly.

'What's that up there?' questioned Jepson, gazing up at the sky.

Bond responded, 'Well, that's what I mean – it's the moon, isn't it?'

Jepson returned, 'And how far away is *that*?'

Bond thought for a minute, and replied, 'It's about two hundred and sixty thousand miles, isn't it?'

Jepson ended the conversation with, 'Then how bloody far do you want to see?'

Brian Johnston:

When Harold Larwood played against Wilfred Rhodes for the first time, he noticed that the Yorkshire batsman, when he was taking his stance, had the front of his left foot cocked off the ground.

'What's he doing that for?' said Lol to umpire Bill Reeves.

'Oh, he always stands like that,' said the umpire.

'He won't to me,' said Larwood, and rushing up to the wicket bowled a full toss, which landed with a mighty crack on Rhodes's toes.

'How's that?' yelled Larwood.

'Bloody painful, I should think!' said Reeves.

Dickie Bird:

I was umpiring at square leg in a county game at Derbyshire and Devon Malcolm, who normally wears glasses but opts for contact lenses when playing, was fielding on the fine-leg boundary. The ball was played down towards him and he raced round – well, ambled is probably a better description, because Devon was no Linford Christie – in order to field it. He threw it in and it hit me smack between the shoulder blades.

I wondered what the hell had happened. I went down like a pricked balloon. Devon ran up to me, concern written all over his face. He picked me up, dusted me down, and muttered, 'Sorry, Dickie, I thought you were the stumps.'

'Dev,' I said, 'I know your eyesight isn't brilliant, mate, but I can't believe that. Whenever did you come across stumps wearing a white cap?'

DOWN UNDER

Darren Gough:

On my first tour of Australia in 1994/95, England took part in a one-day tournament with Australia, an Australian 'A' team and Zimbabwe. After losing our opener against Australia, we went down twice in a single weekend to the Australian Cricket Academy – fortunately, I had a slight hamstring strain – and then to Zimbabwe in Sydney. I didn't play at Toowoomba, where Mike Gatting hit a double hundred before being hit in the mouth while fielding.

Our physio ordered him not to eat that night, but we spotted a couple of empty pizza boxes outside his room. Gatt claimed he'd been framed. That was rich. I remember asking him directions in Sydney. He replied, 'Easy. It's right at the Italian, left at the curry house and just beyond the Chinese!'

Brian Johnston:

On the 1924/25 MCC tour of Australia, Andrew Sandham, the Surrey and England opening batsman, was fielding on the boundary near the famous Hill at the Sydney Cricket Ground. Someone in the crowd kept shouting, 'Sandy, ask your skipper to send out someone else, you're too ugly!'

After this had been going on for some time, Sandham got fed up with it and told his captain, Arthur Gilligan, who suggested that he send Patsy Hendren to field out there. Hendren made his way towards the Hill and had got only halfway there when another shout went up, 'Send back Sandham!'

Michael Parkinson:

Jack Fingleton once told me about the time he first opened for New South Wales with the legendary Charlie Macartney. 'As he walked to the wicket, Macartney said to me, "Now think on, young Fingleton, be ready first ball." I would have done anything for him, but I wasn't sure what he meant. Did he mean be prepared for a quick single? Was he telling me to concentrate from the first moment?

'All these questions were racing through my mind as the fast bowler raced in for the first ball and as he did, I saw Macartney walking down the wicket with his bat at shoulder level.

'In an instant several things happened. The bowler bowled and Macartney, halfway down the wicket, gave it an awesome smack. The bowler dived for cover, so did I. The ball hit the sightscreen on the full and bounced back fifty yards on to the field of play.

'It was the most audacious shot I have ever seen. As I lay there alongside the fast bowler, who was by now a gibbering wreck, I saw the batsman standing above me tapping the wicket with his bat. "Just like I said, young Fingleton. Always ready from the first ball." He looked at the hapless bowler and said confidentially, "They don't like it, you know!"'

Darren Gough:

At the end of the fourth day in the Boxing Day Test at Melbourne in 1994, England were on 79 for 4 and Alec Stewart was coming in at number seven because of a broken finger. The fifth day's play lasted 12.3 overs and produced just 13 runs, as well as a little piece of cricket history. Shane Warne, wicketless up to that point in our second innings, took the first Ashes hat-trick for over ninety years. Phil DeFreitas was the first, lbw playing back. Off I set. At 91 for 7, I'm not sure what my game plan was. It didn't matter. Warnie got one to turn and bounce. I tried to leave it, but Ian Healy took a great catch as it flew off my glove.

As I turned to leave, I suddenly realised what a big

ground the MCG is and what a long way back it was. The stupid duck was quacking on the big screen and the crowd was roaring 'Warnie! Warnie!' at the prospect of their favourite son taking a Test hat-trick on his home ground.

I suppose there is no better sight for a bowler on a hat-trick than seeing Devon Malcolm walk out. In golfing terms, it's the nearest thing you can get to a 'gimme'. As Devon passed me, 'Good luck' was all I could think of to say. He was still fiddling with his thigh pad and gloves. We all knew what was coming – the googly, it had to be. The expected Devon wind-up never came. He pushed forward, the ball hit his glove and David Boon took a magnificent catch at short square. The MCG went wild.

'Why didn't you have a go at him, Dev?'

His reply was pure Devon. 'I was going to, but then I thought I'd play properly.'

Properly! Can you believe it? Shane Warne on a hat-trick and Devon Malcolm thinks he can bat!

Brian Johnston:

A batsman in a match at the Sydney Cricket Ground had played and missed a number of times. Finally, Yabba, the famous Sydney Hill barracker, shouted out to the bowler, 'Send him down a grand piano, and see if he can play *that*!'

Barry Johnston:

In early 1999, Tom Cruise flew out to Australia to film *Mission Impossible 2* for six months at Rupert Murdoch's Fox Studios in Sydney and on location in New South Wales. After shooting finished in September, the Hollywood star stayed on in Sydney with his Australian wife Nicole Kidman and their two adopted children to spend a few months with her family over Christmas.

In the New Year, Australia were taking part in the tri-nation Carlton and United Series, eight one-day internationals with India and Pakistan. Australia were playing India at the Sydney Cricket Ground and the British film director Sam Mendes invited Cruise to join him in his box to watch his first cricket match.

'He didn't know anything about cricket,' said Mendes later. 'I told him about Warne and Tendulkar, how amazing Bradman was, and that Mark Taylor had declared when he was 334 not out, equal with Bradman's Australian Test record.'

He added, 'Tom was so moved, he was practically in tears!'

Michael Parkinson:

Keith Miller had the capacity to talk a leg off an iron pot when the mood took him and I would just listen. He told me this story about Arthur Morris:

'I once bowled him eight bouncers in an over. There had been a lot of discussion in the press about short-pitched bowling. There was a lot of talk about banning it or limiting the number of bouncers, so I thought I'd have a spot of fun.

'When Arthur came out to bat I put nine men on the square-leg boundary and just bowled at his head. When I bowled the first one, Arthur said, "Oh dear, a bouncer." And every time I bowled another, he'd say, "Oh my God, he's done it again." And it so tickled me that I started laughing so much that the tears were running down my face as I came in to bowl. I could hardly make it to the crease. Old Arthur was in a right state.'

'Was Morris all right?' I inquired.

'All right?' said Miller. 'He hit me for thirty-four in the over!'

Brian Johnston:

Godfrey Evans, the Kent and England wicketkeeper, made a particularly good stumping on the leg side when playing in an up-country match on one of his tours of Australia. As he whipped off the bails he shouted to the umpire, 'How's that?'

The umpire replied, 'Bloody marvellous!'

Ian Brayshaw:

A balmy afternoon during a Test match at the Melbourne Cricket Ground was rudely interrupted by a between-overs announcement through the public-address system.

'Would Mr J. Smith of Hawthorn please go home,' the voice announced. 'Your wife is having her baby and must be taken to hospital.'

Laughter flowed around the ground as the spectators pictured a harassed father-to-be hurrying off home to his wife. Not so, however, because after about half an hour the voice again boomed across the ground, this time with some urgency:

'Repeating our earlier message to Mr J. Smith of Hawthorn . . . would he please go home immediately, because his wife is in labour and must be taken to hospital straight away.'

Much more mirth from the crowd, this time picturing a man reluctant to leave the cricket – but surely by now bidding farewell to his mates to dash to his vehicle and tear off home. How wrong were 20,000 spectators! Much to their delight, the now pleading message was repeated with grim urgency some twenty minutes later. After a further thirty minutes had passed, there was a bland announcement:

'Would Mr J. Smith of Hawthorn please go to the Mercy Hospital, where his wife has now given birth to a baby son!'

Brian Johnston:

While he was in Australia with the 1962/63 MCC team, the Reverend David Sheppard came in for more than his fair share of dropped catches. The story was going around that a young English couple, who had settled in Australia, were due to have their first-born christened. The husband suggested that it would be nice if they got David Sheppard to do it for them.

'Oh no,' said the horrified wife, 'not likely, he would only drop it!'

Fred Trueman:

On the 1958/59 MCC tour of Australia I learned a lot about cricket, but also about how Australians view themselves:

- The bigger the hat, the smaller the sheep farm.
- The shorter the nickname, the more they warm to you.
- Whether it is the opening of Parliament in Canberra or a new fine art gallery in Sydney, there is no formal event in Australia that can't be improved by a sausage sizzle.
- They will refer to their best friend as 'a total bastard', whereas their worst enemy is 'a bit of a bastard'.
- When invited to a party, the done thing is to take

along a bottle of cheap red wine that slides down the throat like a rusty knife, then spend the evening drinking the host's tinnies. One should never feel self-conscious about doing that, as the host will expect it from you and will have catered for it.

- When out in the territories, the neon sign advertising the motel's pool will be slightly larger than the pool itself.
- The true mark of the esteem in which an Australian cricketer is held is not having a stand named after him, but a bar in the ground – better still, a urinal, as in 'The Wally Grout Gents' in Sydney.
- The benchmark of a man's masculinity is to erect a beach umbrella in the face of a strong south-easterly.
- The wise person chooses a partner who is not only attractive to them, but also to midges and mosquitoes.

Barry Johnston:

In December 2004, a vital league match between the Inverloch Cricket Club and their local rivals Nerrena in Victoria, Australia, ended in chaos after the visitors were served green-speckled cupcakes during the tea interval. The Nerrena players claimed later that the cakes were laced with marijuana, although the Inverloch club secretary dismissed the allegations as simply 'rumours'.

Nerrena player Tim Clark recalled, 'I thought, gee, this is pretty good, they usually feed us crap.' In fact the cupcakes were so delicious that Clark ate five and two of his team-mates polished off the remainder. Things started to fall apart for the Nerrena side after tea when one player took nearly twenty minutes to put on his pads. The two others kept breaking into hysterical laughter and had to dash off the field during play for drinks of water.

Not surprisingly this extraordinary behaviour un-nerved the rest of the team and Nerrena lost by fifty runs. The two Victorian sides were in a relegation battle at the bottom of their local league and Nerrena were consigned to the second division.

After the match Tim Clark still felt rather light-headed, but he had to assemble a kit bike for a fundraiser that evening. Clark confessed, 'After a small lie-down I tried to follow the instructions, but I was all over the shop. I was putting the handlebars where the seat was meant to be!' When he finally completed the bike, he was four hours late for the club function.

Somehow the three Nerrena players who had scoffed all the cakes managed to drive themselves home, but they had a lucky escape. As one admitted later, if the police had tested him for drugs on the way home and he had come up positive, what could he have told them?

'Sorry, officer. It wasn't me. I was fed drugged cupcakes at the cricket!'

Christopher Martin Jenkins:

The first tour I was lucky enough to make was that famous 1974/75 Ashes tour when Lillee and Thomson were so all dominating and Thommo was the new boy on the block. Max O'Connell, the umpire from Adelaide, swears that after he got an England wicket, Thommo put his sleeveless sweater back on and asked Max how many balls there were left in the over.

Max replied, 'Three.'

Thommo scratched his head and said, 'Is that three gone or three to come?'

Brian Johnston:

There's a lovely cricket story about the late Duke of Norfolk, who went as the manager of Ted Dexter's team to Australia in 1962/63. They loved him in Australia – they called him 'Dukey' – because wherever MCC played he leased a racehorse and ran it in the local meeting.

MCC were playing against South Australia at Adelaide, and about twenty-two miles outside Adelaide there is a racecourse called Gawlor. There's a lovely paddock there with eucalyptus trees and gum trees, very picturesque.

The Duke had a horse running there, so he thought he would go and see it. He spotted it under the eucalyptus tree and walked across the paddock in his pinstriped suit, Panama hat and MCC ribbon, very much the Duke. As he approached, to his horror, he saw the trainer put his hand in his pocket and give the horse something to eat.

He thought, oh, my God, I'm a member of the Jockey Club at home. So he went up to the trainer and said, 'I hope you didn't give him anything you shouldn't have, trainer. We don't want any trouble with dope here.'

'No, no, Your Grace,' said the trainer. 'I just gave him a lump of sugar. I'm going to eat one myself. Would you like one too, Your Grace?'

The Duke thought he'd better humour him, so he ate the lump of sugar, talked about the race and went off to watch it from the grandstand. Five minutes before the race started, in came the jockeys, waddling as they do.

The Duke's jockey went up under the eucalyptus tree to his horse and the trainer said, 'Look. This is a seven-furlong race. The first five furlongs, keep tucked in behind and don't move. But for the last two furlongs, give him all you've got, and if anyone passes you after that, it's either the Duke of Norfolk or myself!'

Fred Trueman:

The Reverend David Sheppard had one or two catching lapses on the 1962/63 MCC tour of Australia. They were all the more poignant to me because they occurred when he was fielding at short fine leg, a position I regarded very definitely as mine. I couldn't field there to my own bowling, of course, and so the future Bishop of Liverpool was occasionally to be found there. Eventually, his mistakes caused him to be moved to *deep* fine leg, and it was there that his moment of triumph came . . . or so he thought. Fred Titmus dropped one short, the batsman hooked, and Sheppard, on the boundary, held the catch.

In a frenzy of delight, he hurled the ball high into the air and, as he waited for the ball to return to his hands, the voice of Brian Statham was heard from the neighbouring third man: 'You'd better chuck it in, Rev. It was a no-ball and they're on their third run!'

Barry Johnston:

The Australian actor and comedian Paul Hogan, star of the 1986 comedy-adventure movie *Crocodile Dundee*, could be relied upon to give an opinion on almost anything. Like his laid-back character Mick Dundee, he believed that life should be enjoyed to the full, and he thought Aussie cricketers were taking the game too seriously.

'Cricket needs brightening up,' Hogan said once. 'My solution is to let the players drink at the beginning of the game, not after. It always works in our picnic matches!'

Brian Johnston:

It was a Sunday during the MCC tour of Australia in 1928/29. Patsy Hendren and Percy Chapman, the England captain, decided to get away from it all and they borrowed a car for a run into the country. After a few miles they went round a corner and saw a cricket match about to start in a field adjoining the road. As all cricketers are wont to do, they stopped the car with the intention of watching the game for a few minutes. The car had no sooner stopped than an Australian strolled over and said, 'Do either of you chaps play cricket?'

Chapman pointed to Hendren and said, 'He plays a little.'

'Good oh,' said the fellow, 'we are a man short. Will you make up for us?'

Although it was Patsy's day off he obliged, and as his adopted side were fielding the captain sent him out to long on. Patsy went to the allotted position, and as the field was on a slope he was out of sight of the pitch. He had nothing to do except throw the ball in occasionally. He was lost to sight for a long time when at last a towering hit was sent in his direction. Patsy caught the ball and ran up the hill shouting, 'I caught it, I caught it.'

The batsman looked at him with daggers drawn – it was *his* captain. 'You lunatic . . . they were out twenty minutes ago. *We* are batting now!'

Ian Brayshaw:

The Indian cricket team made a most disappointing start to its three-Test series in Australia in 1980/81. The tourists went down by an innings in the First Test, which began in Sydney just after Christmas. The margin was largely due to a fighting double century by Australian Greg Chappell, but aided by some most irresponsible strokeplay by the Indians.

After the game, the Indian captain Sunil Gavaskar was asked for his comments on the ignominious defeat. The little fellow forced a smile and said, 'We gave away our wickets like Christmas presents . . . trouble is, we Indians don't celebrate Christmas!'

Barry Johnston:

In 1971 anti-apartheid protestors disrupted a South African rugby union tour of Australia. There were several angry disturbances and the Australian Cricket Board decided at the last minute to cancel a tour by South Africa planned for later that year. Instead, they invited a Rest of the World XI, under the captaincy of Garry Sobers, to play a five-Test series against Australia.

Before the First Test in Brisbane, the members of the Rest of the World team were met at the airport by a group of Australian officials. One of the Rest of the World players was the young South-African-born Tony Greig, who would make his England debut the following year. Greig was introduced to an elderly gentleman by his team-mate and fellow countryman Hilton Ackerman, who then left them alone. Greig didn't quite get the old man's name and spent a few minutes making small talk. Then he asked the elderly gentleman to hold his bag while he went to the toilet.

When Greig returned, he sat down and, since the other man was very quiet, he tried to make some polite conversation with him. He asked him if he was with the Australian Board and the elderly gentleman replied yes, he was. Then Greig asked him if he had himself played any cricket in his life, to which the elderly gentleman also answered, 'Yes.'

Still none the wiser, Greig said, 'I'm sorry, but I didn't get your name.'

The elderly gentleman replied, 'Donald Bradman.'

Barry Johnston:

When Dennis Lillee and Jeff Thomson were at the height of their fame they were interviewed together on Australian television. At one point the interviewer asked Lillee, 'Tell me, Dennis, what would you do if you discovered you had only thirty minutes to live?'

Lillee replied, 'I'd make love to the first thing that moved!'

The interviewer turned to Thomson, 'And what would you do, Jeff?'

'Thommo' replied, 'I wouldn't move for half an hour!'

OFF THE FIELD

Barry Johnston:

In the early 2000s, the great Australian wicketkeeper-batsman Adam Gilchrist was browsing in the bookshop at Adelaide airport, waiting for a flight. As often happens with international cricketers, especially when they are as famous as Gilchrist in Australia, he could feel that someone was staring at him, probably hoping for an autograph.

Sure enough, a few moments later a man came up to him and tapped him on the shoulder.

'Excuse me, mate,' he said, 'but aren't you Glenn McGrath?'

At this point, Gilchrist admits to feeling slightly foolish for believing that everyone knew who he was, so he answered politely, 'No, I'm not Glenn McGrath.'

He paused, wondering if the man would now realise his mistake.

Instead, the man said, 'Oh bummer,' and walked off!

Dickie Bird:

In a county match, Lancashire were playing Northamptonshire at Northampton. The match had finished and it was the last day. We were all coming off the field when Allan Lamb came up and shook hands with me. He said, 'Thanks for the game, Dickie. All the best. Have a good journey home.'

I said, 'Thank you, Lamby. See you later in the season.'

I had my shower, got changed, and went into the car park to get my car to drive home. I couldn't believe what I saw. He'd taken all four wheels off my car. It was jacked up. My wheels were at the side of the railings and he'd put a big notice on the windscreen: ALL THE BEST, DICKIE. HAVE A GOOD JOURNEY HOME!

Jonathan Agnew:

One morning in 2000, I found myself in a room at Buckingham Palace waiting to interview His Royal Highness Prince Philip the Duke of Edinburgh. This was the fiftieth anniversary of the Lord's Taverners, the well-known charity founded by some actors in the Lord's Tavern in 1950, which raises money to help disabled and disadvantaged children play sport, and cricket in particular.

Prince Philip had been their Patron – or twelfth man,

as he was known – since the very start, and it had been arranged by the BBC that I should interview him as part of a programme to celebrate the work of the Taverners for Radio 5 Live. We had been allocated half an hour of the Prince's time, and had been told to submit our ten questions in advance for his approval and, presumably, his preparation.

With a producer and a sound man, who set up the recording equipment, I waited in the Duke's office, the walls of which were entirely covered from floor to ceiling with bookshelves. There was a desk, and a couple of chairs and a sofa beside a table. It was nine o'clock in the morning – which meant I had been up very early to catch the six o'clock train from Leicester – and we were the Duke's first appointment of the day.

The door opened, and I could hear a muttered conversation and a rustle of paper, which sounded like an adviser showing him our questions. At last the Duke, rather stooped, walked busily into his office. Brief introductions and perfunctory handshakes followed, and he motioned me to sit opposite him for the interview.

As a means of providing a sound check for the engineer, I explained what the programme was all about, and we were ready to go. I read out the first question on the sheet, which from memory asked the Duke how he first became involved with the charity. He gave a rather vague reply, of no more than five seconds. A little flustered, I moved on to the next question, which was met by an equally brief response, and on we went.

After a minute and a half it was all over; I had asked all ten questions. Glancing up from the sheet of paper, I saw my producer in the background, his shoulders heaving in silent mirth. With that the Duke rose from his chair, said goodbye and left the room as briskly as he had entered only moments earlier!

A little chastened and armed with an unusable interview, the three of us walked through the gates of Buckingham Palace and headed to the nearest underground station, only to discover that it was closed because of a bomb scare, as was my line to St Pancras. It had been a frustrating yet, curiously, rather an amusing day.

I met the Duke again in 2009, at a dinner in London hosted by CCPR, the alliance of governing and representative bodies of sport and recreation in the United Kingdom. Tim Lamb, the former head of the England and Wales Cricket Board, was the chief executive of the CCPR, and he introduced me to Prince Philip, who was attending his final dinner as President after fifty-eight years in the role.

'You'll know Jonathan, sir,' said Tim. 'He commentates on *Test Match Special* on the radio.'

'Never listen,' replied the Duke gruffly. 'They never give the score!'

As he moved away, all I could manage was a disappointingly obsequious, 'Thank you, sir . . .'

Min Patel:

You would think Michael Holding would know his way around the UK, having spent numerous summers on the county circuit with Derbyshire, then later as a television pundit. But when he was commentating on the fourth West Indies v England Test at Old Trafford in 1995, he was still unsure how to negotiate the approximately two-mile drive from the Copthorne Hotel in Salford Quays to the ground.

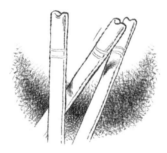

Then Mikey had a moment of pure genius. He would follow one of the England team (who were also in residence there) to the ground. Spotting a certain G.A. Hick heading out of the front doors, Michael sped to his car.

It was about an hour later, while heading south down the M6 at a fair lick, that it dawned on the Windies speedster that Hick had been left out of the final eleven and was heading home to Worcester!

Henry Blofeld:

I first saw Alec Bedser bowl in 1948, when he got Don Bradman out twice in his last Test match at Lord's. He went on to be an England selector and he was chairman of the selectors during the 1970s, but he didn't enjoy the new-fangled cricket. I suppose that's only natural. It was a very different game from the one he'd played.

Alec told me a lovely story about when he was chairman of the selectors. It was in 1975, the year of the first World Cup, when the Australians stayed on and played four Test matches. Alec didn't go near the dressing room during the game, but after every day's play he used to go in and talk to the captain, Tony Greig. They'd have a bit of a chat about tactics and what they were going to do the next day.

After the second day's play at The Oval in the Fourth Test, Alec went in to see Greig and while they were chatting, Alec heard this extraordinary whirring noise behind him. He said to Greig, 'Captain, what's that whirring noise?'

Greig looked over his shoulder and replied, 'Oh, that's Bob Woolmer's hairdryer.'

Alec said, 'Hairdryer? Hairdryer! What's wrong with a bleedin' towel?'

Justin Langer:

In the Third Test against Pakistan at Sharjah, in 2002, I was fielding at bat-pad on the third day when Pakistan's middle-order batsman Hasan Raza pounced on a short ball from Warney and hit it straight at me. I instinctively turned away but was struck on the back of the head, and dropped like a lead balloon. I'd been hit a few times before, but this one was like the lights going out, even though I was wearing a helmet. Apparently, I was unconscious on the ground for two minutes before I got up and walked, dazed and nauseous, to the changing rooms.

Our medical staff were worried and decided to get me to hospital for a precautionary brain scan, and that's when my problems really began. They put me in a neck brace on a stretcher. As the attendants were loading me into the ambulance, they pushed a bit hard and I whacked my head on the wall inside it.

With our security officer, Reg Dickason, in the back with me, we headed off down the highway to the hospital in Dubai. The driver completely ignored the speed humps, sending me bouncing on the stretcher in the back every time we went over one at 100 kilometres per hour. By the time we got to the hospital, I reckon my concussion was actually worse than when I was hit in the head.

Reg went off to see the hospital administrators but the ambulance officers had other ideas. They unloaded me, still on the stretcher, and tried to wheel me into an elevator that was clearly too small for the trolley. In their vain attempts to squeeze me into the lift, they kept banging my head against the elevator wall – until they gave up and tried the stairwell instead. Ignoring my pleas to stop, they ended up carrying me up this stair-case, my head pointing down and banging against the stretcher rails.

Reg reappeared, realised what was going on and started yelling at these two clowns. Eventually, they loaded me back into the ambulance and took me back to Sharjah to another hospital, where the brain scans thank-fully revealed nothing wrong other than concussion – mostly caused by the trip!

Christopher Martin-Jenkins:

There is nothing like playing cricket and when you love it as much as I do, you find it hard not see cricket in almost everything. It was said of Canon Edward Lyttelton, of the great Lyttelton cricketing family, that he could never quite go down the knave of Norwich Cathedral without wondering if it would take spin!

Ian Botham:

I have many great memories of touring with the England team during my cricket career, and numerous stories to tell about my room-mates! However, one man stands out in particular – Derek Randall, or 'Arkle' as he is known to his fellow players and friends.

On returning to his hotel room in Adelaide, following a day in the field, he decided to run a bath. Having turned the water on, he remembered that he needed to pass on a message to Messrs I.T. Botham and A.J. Lamb. He quickly wrapped a towel around his body and slipped across the corridor to our room. We opened the door to Arkle, invited him in for a drink (a cup of Earl Grey, of course) and spent a while chatting. On leaving, he realised that he had left his key inside his own room. Unlike most people, instead of asking either Lamby or myself to ring down to reception, he decided to go down himself.

At the Adelaide Hilton that night, there was a rather special function, with people from all over Australia arriving dressed in DJs – the works. As the towel-clad Arkle arrived at the reception desk, there was utter chaos, with people running hell for leather out of the dining room, some soaking wet.

While asking the very flustered receptionist if he could have another key for his room, he also inquired what the problem was.

'Some stupid **** has left their bath water running and flooded the dining area!'

No need to ask who, as she handed over the replacement key to a slightly under-dressed Mr Randall!

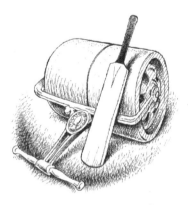

Barry Johnston:

In 2007, Sir Ian Botham was a guest on chef Gordon Ramsay's Channel 4 series *The F Word*. He took part in the Cliff Richard Celebrity Wine Challenge, so-called because Sir Cliff had been so bad at it. In a blind tasting, Botham had to try two different wines and decide which was the good wine and which was the celebrity plonk. He considers himself to be a wine connoisseur and even has his own label wine, which is produced in South Australia.

Much to his embarrassment, Botham failed the first taste test miserably, preferring Barry Manilow's cheaper Chardonnay at £10 a bottle to a Bâtard-Montrachet

Grand Cru at £106 a bottle, which he said was undrinkable. Gordon Ramsay commented harshly that Botham and Barry Manilow shared the same nose for wine!

Botham did better on the second test, choosing a Chateau Montrose Cabernet Sauvignon 1996 at £70 over a bottle of Madonna's own label wine at £20. Finally, Sir Ian salvaged some of his reputation when he correctly picked his own wine, a Botham Merrill Willis Cabernet Sauvignon over the alternative, which he declared to be absolutely 'shocking'.

Unfortunately for Sir Cliff Richard, it was a bottle of *his* own label wine, Vida Nova!

Jimmy Anderson:

Though pranks are slightly a thing of the past, I do still look back with fondness on the days when they were popular. Our security guy Reg Dickason was, and still is, usually involved in some shape or form. Ian Bell once superglued his shoes to the floor; it must have taken him a long time to do it. That was quite an interesting battle!

Mark Saxby, the physio/resident DJ, had a camper van, the old-school Volkswagen, that he used to park at the school across from The Oval. Reg filled the entire camper van with scrunched-up newspaper – Mark couldn't get into it!

The Yorkshire team once had a phenomenon called

the 'Yorkshire Snipper'. Someone would cut the toes of your socks off or the crotch from your undies. It became an epidemic. No one ever knew who it was. They ended up having a serious team meeting about it. David Byas, the captain then, said, 'We're not leaving the dressing room till someone owns up to this,' but the Yorkshire Snipper called his bluff and never owned up.

Myth has it that he took on more than one identity eventually. Particularly inspired, and at the time a bit of a cheeky upstart, Joe Root brought him into the England team. You'd come back from lunch and all your stuff had holes in it.

Joe would be terrible at hiding it. He'd just go bright red and have a stupid grin on his face!

Justin Langer:

Part of the rigmarole of being a Test cricketer is meeting dignitaries and attending formal events. Some are memorable, others pass you by. The dignitary who made the most positive impression on me was Queen Elizabeth II. I met Her Majesty twice and I'll never forget either occasion. The first time was on the 1997 Ashes tour at Buckingham Place.

Mark Taylor, our captain, escorted Her Majesty along the row of players. The closer she inched to me, the more nervous I got, until there she was standing in front of me. Sometimes on occasions such as this, you notice that the person shaking your hand has already moved their eyesight along to the next person in the line. I never take it as an insult, although it is disconcerting, and it confirms that they are doing a job rather than enjoying the experience. The Queen was different. As she took my hand, she looked me straight in the eyes. For those few seconds I felt quite special, as if she was really interested in meeting me.

Afterwards we had tea and scones. The Queen stayed and kept chatting. I found myself in a circle with her while she talked to Mark Waugh about racehorses. Probably I got too relaxed and plucked up too much courage, because a short while later I found myself talking to Prince Andrew and asking him if I could pose a question.

'Anything,' the prince said.

'Do you know every room in the palace?'

The prince looked at me for a few seconds. Then he replied with a question of his own.

'Do you know every room in *your* house?'

That put me in my place!

Joe Root:

It was a nice surprise when I was awarded the Compton-Miller Medal for being Man of the Series in the 2015

Ashes. To be fair, Stuart Broad was deserving of something too, having finished up as the leading wicket-taker, with twenty-one. He was to get an altogether different surprise, however, as the dressing-room snipper made a final incision for the summer.

Sock snipping appeared to undergo something of a rebirth that Ashes series, as there was a phantom snipper, or perhaps multiple snippers, on the loose in the England dressing room. In fact, the epidemic was so bad by the time we got to The Oval for the Fifth Test that I broke an old Yorkshire pledge and put my hand in my pocket, forking out for a present for the rest of the lads – I popped into Top Man and bought twenty pairs of socks and stockpiled them in the middle of the dressing room.

Anyone pointing the finger at me can be assured that not only did I have my socks snipped after the Fourth Test at Trent Bridge, but someone took the scissors to my boxer shorts as well. It became something of a free-for-all throughout the summer, with everybody getting hacked on a weekly basis. There were a number of prime suspects, but like any fair judicial system, we worked on the basis that everyone is innocent until they are found guilty.

Throughout the series, Broad had made it clear to everyone not to go near his lucky pair of green socks. They were to be tampered with on pain of death.

Therefore, there had been a good amount of restraint shown towards him for the previous six weeks.

After the final Test at The Oval, we invited the Australian team to share a few beers with us in our dressing room. Later that evening, our celebrations were winding down and there were only a few lads left waiting for their cabs back to the team hotel and Broad was one of that dwindling number. With the socks out of bounds, the opportunity had been seized to take the scissors to another item amongst his belongings – unbeknown to him, a huge hole had been cut out of the bottom of his holdall. As it had been standing upright in the hours after the game, he was none the wiser.

Only when he came to pick it up, throwing both straps over his shoulders, did his parting gift become clear!

Ben Stokes:

After England won the World Cup at Lord's in July 2019, I was dragged away from the celebrations several times during the course of the hour or so after the match. Obviously, after I had done well in the game, everybody wanted to speak to me. I understood that. But quite honestly, it's the last thing you want to do. You just want to be with your team, all together sharing the experience. Making memories.

This was the time to savour our success as a group,

and also to share it with our friends and families, who sacrifice lots for our careers. We invited them to join us in the middle of the ground, and as the sun sank behind the pavilion, it was some start to the after-party. It was so nice to have everyone enjoying each other's success.

From there, we took things into the home dressing room, where we would get the chance to reflect on our achievement and allow it to sink in. Within two minutes of leaving the hallowed turf to relocate, however, I was asked to speak to the written press by Danny Reuben, the England team's media manger.

Bear in mind, I have always been one to enjoy toasting the team's successes, let alone a World Cup Final win, so I got Andy, one our security guys, in on a plan to get out of this request.

'I am going to act like I've had a few,' I told him.

Truth was that I was only on my second beer, but I reckoned there was no way Danny would let me do it if I was slurring my words.

Thankfully, Andy is a Leeds lad and pretty chilled: 'I'll do whatever you want, mate.'

So I went down from the second-floor dressing room to the ground with Andy, wearing no shoes or socks, swaying from side to side, eyes rolling around in their sockets.

'Reubs, am I really doing more media in this state? Are

you, the England media manager, going to put me in front of the cameras like this?'

Sam Dickason, one of our senior security team, was with him. He didn't know I was putting it on either and the pair of them fell for it.

'You're off the hook, get back upstairs,' Sam instructed me.

Undoubtedly, that was one of the best moves I'd pulled off throughout the entire World Cup!

SLEDGING

Barry Johnston:

In the Centenary Test at Melbourne in 1977, David Hookes was making his Test debut for Australia. As he made his way out to the crease, the twenty-one-year-old was met by the England captain, South-African-born Tony Greig, who asked the fair-haired young batsman, 'When are your balls going to drop, sonny?'

Hookes replied, 'I don't know, but at least I'm playing cricket for my own country!'

Matthew Hayden:

I've dished it out and I've copped it back. I've locked horns with some of the game's biggest names, and I've been on the receiving end of sledges from little old ladies, family members and even priests. In fact, one of the most memorable sledges came from someone who was both a family member *and* a priest – my mum's late brother, Father Pat Jones.

Father Pat was the parish priest at Weipa when I visited

the North Queensland town for a Super 8's game early in my career. After watching me play out a pretty docile first over, he roared from the bleachers, 'Do you mind playing a shot? I have to live in this town!'

Richie Benaud:

The closest I reckon I got to experiencing sledging was during the Fourth Ashes Test at Old Trafford in 1956. This will always be remembered as 'Laker's Match' after the England off-spinner finished with the amazing figures of 19 for 90. There were some very unhappy Australians in that match, in the main because we had the feeling we were playing on a rather unusual pitch, and we were looking at defeat, which never actually makes one happy.

Well, you would be unhappy too if you were thrashed, one of the opposition bowlers took nineteen wickets in the match and the ball turned square for much of the game. Additionally, the rain fell on either side of the ground on the last day, but none fell on it. You would also be unhappy if you were the bowler who took only one wicket of the twenty little Australians to fall. Jim Burke was the generous batsman who was the victim of Tony Lock.

On the final afternoon I was engaged in some prudent 'gardening' against 'Lockie', patting down the pitch, sometimes not quite ready to face up, so much so that one prominent English administrator, sitting alongside a very prominent Australian administrator, said grimly that, because of the gardening, I should never at any time in the future hold a position of responsibility in an Australian team.

Out in the centre at Old Trafford, Colin McDonald and I were battling our way through to the tea interval and, in the last over, Tony bowled from what was then the Warwick Road End. I played forward firmly to a half-volley and it went to the bowler's left hand.

Great fielder, 'Lockie', and a very good and accurate throwing arm in either the infield or farther out. He gathered this ball and it rocketed into Godfrey Evans's left glove, alongside my left ear, and floating down the pitch came, 'Tap that one down, you little bastard!'

Barry Johnston:

Ian Botham was the target of a classic sledge by the Australian wicketkeeper Rodney Marsh during the thrilling 1981 Ashes series. As the England all-rounder took guard in one of the Test matches, Marsh tried to put him off by saying, 'So, how's your wife, and my kids?'

Botham silenced him with the brilliant reply, 'The wife's fine . . . but the kids are retarded!'

Michael Atherton:

During my second Test match, at The Oval in 1989, I had my first taste of Australian sledging. They tended to pick on the youngest, or those they considered the weakest. Merv Hughes probably thought I was both young and weak and he snarled at me constantly through his ludicrous moustache. He was all bristle and bullshit and I couldn't make out what he was saying, except that every sledge ended with 'arsewipe'. I smiled and shrugged and saved my energy.

Two years later, in the First Test against Australia at Old Trafford, I made 19 and 25 and I was once again a verbal target for Merv Hughes. I had not played against him since the previous Ashes series and had missed his kind and gentle countenance. As I nicked the first ball for four through third man the moustache hissed at me, 'Jesus Christ, you've not got any better in two f***ing years!' And then as I ran past him, just in case I had forgotten his calling card, he added, '. . . arsewipe!'

Barry Johnston:

During a county championship match between Glamorgan and Somerset, Greg Thomas was bowling to Viv Richards. The Glamorgan paceman had managed to beat the bat a couple of times and was feeling rather pleased with himself. He taunted Richards, 'It's red, round and weighs about five ounces, in case you were wondering.'

The next delivery, Viv Richards took an almighty heave at the ball and smashed it straight out of the ground and into a river – after which he turned to Thomas and said, 'Greg, you know what it looks like. Now go and find it!'

Shane Warne:

England have generally begun each Ashes series against us with plenty to say for themselves. The problem is that if you start sledging without being able to back up your words with performances, then it soon loses its effect. There is no point threatening this and that if you're going to be rissoled inside three days. Merv Hughes in particular used to relish the Ashes contests, and usually reserved a special word for Graeme Hick. England used to say the odd word here and there, but nothing that badly affected any of us.

On the other hand, they could be susceptible themselves. My dismissal of Nasser Hussain, in the first Carlton & United final match at Sydney in 1999, springs to mind. England needed less than 50 to win, with six wickets and 10 overs remaining, and Hussain was going pretty well. He had the reputation of being a little on the fiery side and I decided the only way we could win from that position was to tempt him into doing something silly.

At that stage he was not a regular feature of their one-day side, so I tried to goad him by talking him through the game. I would say things like, 'This is where it's crucial not to get out, Nass,' or, 'Don't let your team-mates down now, mate.'

This went on for a couple of overs and he said a bit back, so it was game on. When he ran down the pitch and hit me over the top, I clapped him and said, 'Great stuff, Nass, that's the way to do it.' At the end of the over his face was red and you could almost see the steam coming out of his ears. I knew then that the ploy might work.

Lo and behold, in my next over he ran down the track, and was stumped by Adam Gilchrist about three yards out of his ground. With new batsmen in, we had a chance. Adam Hollioake followed next ball, and we ended up winning the game. It was one of the few occasions sledging worked – remember, pick your moment!

Barry Johnston:

In 1989 Merv Hughes was bowling to England batsman Robin Smith during the Second Ashes Test at Lord's. After Smith had played and missed several times, Hughes snarled, 'You can't f***ing bat!'

A few balls later, Smith smacked Hughes to the boundary and called out to the fiery Australian, 'Hey, Merv, we make a fine pair. I can't f***ing bat and you can't f***ing bowl!'

Michael Vaughan:

Shane Warne's record speaks for itself. He comes at you even when he is not bowling, standing at first slip chirping away. He is a very psychological player and tries to get into a batsman's head, forever trying to talk players out. Not only that, but he tells you how he is going to get you out. Rather than speaking to the captain in a discreet manner, he will make sure you can hear him. He is one of their best chirpers. He will say things like, 'Don't worry, he's going to hit one straight to gully in a minute.' Comments like that I can just laugh off, but with an inexperienced player it might work, because Warne is quite clever at it.

Not all his plans follow the script. I remember once in Adelaide, he was bowling at Nasser Hussain and said, 'I'm going to throw one up, and you'll drive and edge it.' Two overs later he lobbed one up and, sure enough, Nasser edged it, but just as Warne was about to celebrate and say told you so, Damien Martyn dropped the catch!

Barry Johnston:

Glenn McGrath was bowling to the Zimbabwe number eleven, Eddo Brandes, a heavily built chicken farmer who became famous in 1997 when he took a hat-trick in a one-day international against England. Brandes, nick-named 'Chicken George', was flailing away with his bat, hardly making any contact with the ball, but the Australians could not prise him from the crease. After a few overs, McGrath got so frustrated that he walked up to the Zimbabwean batsman and shouted at him, 'Why are you so fat?'

Quick as a flash, Brandes replied, 'Because every time I make love to your wife, she gives me a biscuit!'

Matthew Hayden:

It's only fair to note that I wasn't always the aggressor where sledging was concerned. Adam Gilchrist loves the story about Holland's wicketkeeper John Smid giving me both barrels at consecutive World Cups in 2003 and 2007. I can remember him saying things like, 'We haven't flown halfway round the world to watch you. Get a single and get Gilly on strike, because you are crap.' This from a Dutch wicketkeeper! Do you mind?

My all-time favourite sledge came at the SCG, in a one-day match against New Zealand during the 2004/05 season. We'd won the toss and batted first, and I had made a respectable 43 off 65 balls. Solid enough by traditional standards, but with Cyclone Gilly blowing palm trees out of the ground at the other end, it seemed like a funeral procession to the fans. Or one fan, at least.

When we started fielding, I was posted to the square-leg fence, and from high up in the Doug Walters Stand I could hear a voice saying, ''Ey, 'Ayden. Yer batting is crap!' He kept asking me if I could hear him, but I didn't want to give him the satisfaction of a reply. My plan was going well until he bellowed out like a bull, 'And 'Ayden, by the way, yer chicken casserole tastes like crap!'

It cracked me up. I could no longer ignore him. I spun on my heel and shouted back, 'Well, you bought the book, you mug. Thanks for the thirty bucks! I'll have a beer on *you* tonight!'

Barry Johnston:

A few weeks before the start of the 2005 Ashes series, Australian all-rounder Shane Watson learned that his fiancée, professional dancer Kym Johnson, had left him for the hunky TV presenter Tom Williams, her partner on the Australian television show *Dancing with the Stars*.

In June, England were playing Australia in their first NatWest Series one-day match at Bristol, when Kevin Pietersen smashed Watson over the boundary for an almighty six, depositing the ball ten rows back, on his way to an unbeaten 91 and an England victory. At the end of the over the blond, spiky-haired Watson started to give Pietersen a dose of the verbals, until KP shut him up by saying, 'You're just upset because no one loves you anymore!'

Even Aussie captain Ricky Ponting chuckled at that one as Watson stomped off to square leg.

Kevin Pietersen:

Sledging, or mental disintegration as the Australians like to call it, is a feature of cricket that fascinates people. What some people don't realise is that sledging can be very humorous too. It's not all swearing and unpleasantness, believe me. What I always try to remember is that it's just playacting.

Before the 2005 Ashes series there was a triangular one-day series between England, Australia and Bangladesh. We won our first two matches but Australia started to find their feet in the day–night game we played at Durham when they beat us by 57 runs, after we had made a very poor start with the bat. Even in defeat, though, we managed to score a few psychological points and have a good laugh in the process, when Darren Gough decided to have a bit of fun at the expense of Aussie all-rounder Shane Watson. The papers had been full of stories of the Aussies being haunted by ghosts at their Lumley Castle hotel overlooking the ground, an opportunity Goughy found too hard to resist.

When Watson, who apparently had not been too keen to be alone in his 'haunted' room, came in to bat, Darren crept up behind him and, in true Scooby-Doo style, went '*Whooooh!*'

Barry Johnston:

Shane Watson was so spooked by the tales of seven-hundred-year-old ghosts at the Lumley Castle hotel that he had to sleep on the floor in Brett Lee's room. England spinner Ashley Giles chortled, 'The thought of big, strapping Shane Watson asking Brett Lee if he could kip on his floor because he was scared of a ghost shows the Aussies are not as big and tough as some people make out.'

When Watson came in to bat at the Riverside Ground next day, Darren Gough welcomed him with the words: 'Don't worry, you can sleep in *my* bed tonight!'

Ben Stokes:

I had two battles on my Test debut. Oh, well, I suppose you should start as you mean to go on. The first was with Brad Haddin.

It was during the Second Test in Adelaide on the 2013/14 Ashes tour. I was having one of those frustrating spells. I was really annoyed with myself. Haddin had just reached his 50 and I managed to bowl a good ball, which he nicked, and wicketkeeper Matt Prior caught it. It was my first Test wicket. Wow! Now I was absolutely on fire. I felt mint.

It was not until Hadds was halfway off the field that umpire Marais Erasmus began checking for a no-ball, and I was like, 'Oh, no, oh no, oh no!' I can't describe how angry I was when it was confirmed that I had over-stepped. How had I done that? I felt like an idiot.

So the last thing I needed was for Haddin, with his annoying cheeky grin, to say, 'That's your first and last Test wicket!'

Eh? I was already devastated. I didn't need that. To say it hit a nerve was an understatement. Of course, I now ran in even harder, looking up at the speed gun every ball to make sure I was hustling him.

I was at boiling point, and Erasmus knew it, stopping me from carrying on my walk towards my opponent at the end of the over, as I gave him a good old spray. I was so pumped up, I couldn't hold back. I kept chirping away, and others, without my knowledge, joined in too.

Jimmy Anderson stood at slip, off Graeme Swann, and he and Matt Prior had their own fun.

'Hadds, I wouldn't get yourself much further into this one with him, mate,' Jimmy said.

'Why, mate?'

'Well, he doesn't quite know the difference between on and off the pitch – if you know what I mean?'

'Nutter,' said Prior.

'Yeah, he's the type of bloke who, if he saw you in a nightclub, wouldn't care about who he was, who you were, or where you both were. He'd just run across the dance floor and headbutt you.'

I was oblivious to all of this. But, I kid you not, I didn't hear another peep from Haddin that match!

Barry Johnston:

During a Test match, Fred Trueman forced an edge from the batsman and it flew straight towards Raman Subba Row standing at first slip. Not only did Subba Row fail to catch it, but the ball went right through his legs and carried on down to the third-man boundary. Trueman was silently fuming as he trudged back to his mark. At the end of the over, Subba Row, looking suitably embarrassed, went up to the bowler and said apologetically, 'Sorry, Fred. I should've kept my legs together.'

Trueman snorted, 'Not you, son. Your mother should've!'

Michael Atherton:

In Melbourne on the 1998/99 Ashes tour, Mark Butcher had moved down to number three from his usual opening berth, but each innings he was in by the second over. Ian Healy, the Australian wicketkeeper, gleefully piped up, 'Not much different at number three, is it, Butch!'

Barry Johnston:

After making his Test debut in 2006, Monty Panesar quickly became a cult hero amongst England cricket fans. The left-arm spinner was the first Sikh to play cricket for England and his exuberant celebrations every time he took a wicket, coupled with his often inept fielding and batting performances, endeared him to spectators and to the public at large. He soon acquired the nickname 'The Sikh of Tweak', although Henry Blofeld once called him Monty Python by mistake on *Test Match Special*.

Before the 2006/07 Ashes series in Australia, Monty went to see a sports psychologist to prepare himself for the tour. He was worried about the sledging he might receive from the Australian players, and also the crowds, because of his poor batting and fielding. His session with the mind doctor seems to have worked. When he was asked what he thought about the Aussie sledging, Monty replied cheerfully, 'Sledging? I'm just glad they've heard of me!'

Richie Benaud:

For straightforward repartee I've always liked David Steele, who was brought into the England team in 1975 by Tony Greig after he took over the captaincy from Mike Denness. When, in the first innings, Barry Wood was lbw to Dennis Lillee with the score at 10 and the very grey-haired right-hander from Northamptonshire arrived in the centre, it was to hear someone chiding Dennis for not having mentioned his father was playing in the match.

It is said Steele looked straight past the Australian wicketkeeper Rodney Marsh and muttered, 'Take a good look at this arse of mine; you'll see plenty of it this summer.' Test innings of 50, 45, 73, 92, 39 and 66, and then a century for Northants against Australia later in the summer, made it a nice little story, some say apocryphal – except that, for whatever extraordinary selection quirk, he never played against Australia again!

Andrew Strauss:

Steve Kirby, the nutty Gloucester opening bowler, once famously sledged Mike Atherton by saying he had seen better players in his fridge!

Barry Johnston:

England were playing Australia and Nasser Hussain was at the crease. Steve Waugh, the Aussie captain, walked over to Ricky Ponting and told him, 'Field at silly point. I want you right under his nose.'

On hearing this, the wicketkeeper Ian Healy blurted out, 'That could be anywhere inside a three-mile radius!'

Nasser couldn't stop himself laughing. He didn't find it quite so funny when he was out three balls later!

Sometimes sledging has the opposite effect to the one intended. After their Ashes triumph in 2005, the members of the England team were each awarded the MBE, including Paul Collingwood, although he played in only one Test and made just seven runs.

A year later it was a different story as England were whitewashed 5–0 in Australia. In the Fifth Test at the Sydney Cricket Ground in January 2007, Shane Warne was making his final Test appearance. Early in his innings he gloved a ball off Monty Panesar and was caught behind, but umpire Aleem Dar turned down the appeal. After that Warne started to receive some heavy sledging from the England fielders, led by Paul Collingwood, who was heard to say, 'Did you get stuck into all the pies and soft drinks over Christmas, Shane?'

Warne responded, 'You aren't putting me off, you know. You're making me concentrate even more.'

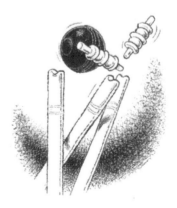

At one point the constant chirping from the England fielders became so animated that umpire Billy Bowden had to intervene, but it backfired on England. Warne, now fired-up by all the banter, smashed 71 off just 65 balls to put Australia firmly in command of the match. As he sent another six sailing into the stands, Warne turned to Collingwood and said, 'You got an MBE right? For scoring seven at The Oval. How embarrassing is that?'

The undisputed winner on points – Mr Shane Warne.

SUMMARISERS

Daniel Norcross:

The first time I commentated on a men's Test match was at Edgbaston in 2016. I was privileged to share the box with that legendary genius of commentary, Henry Blofeld. Blowers was getting a bit long in the tooth by then and was having a little trouble with his eyesight. So much so that for two overs he confused the stocky Zimbabwe-born, England left-hander Gary Ballance with the lithe British Asian Moeen Ali, who was sporting his iconic beard.

'Ballance is batting far more flamboyantly than we're used to seeing,' Blowers said during one over, followed by, 'Moeen is adopting a far more crab-like stance. He's playing the ball unusually deep in his crease. It's all rather unusual.'

He was on commentary with Graeme Swann, who is a great talker and likes to get involved, but on this occasion he wasn't sure whether he should correct the great man.

Now Blowers is very much from the old school of radio commentary in which the ball-by-ball commentator talks through the over and then hands over to his colour man to sum up what has just happened in the last six balls. Seeing Swannie getting a bit fidgety during the over, Blowers started describing in minute detail a man he could see over 100 metres away in the Eric Hollies Stand 'wearing a quite fabulous pair of cerise-coloured trousers, and he appears to be playing some sort of game with a young man I assume is his grandson.'

When Blowers came off commentary I asked him, with genuine awe, how he had managed to spot such a tiny detail in the crowd from so far away.

'Oh, my dear old thing,' he chuckled, 'there was no man in cerise trousers. I just wanted to shut Swannie up!'

Barry Johnston:

The two main summarisers on *Test Match Special* throughout the 1970s and 1980s were Fred Trueman and Trevor Bailey, the former Essex and England all-rounder. Trevor was a useful man to have in the commentary box because, unlike almost everyone else, he was able to keep a straight face. His nickname was 'Boil', which led to an unfortunate slip of the tongue when Brian Johnston introduced him one day, announcing, 'I'm joined by the Balls . . . I mean, the Boil!'

During another Test match there was a discussion in the box about whether a particular captain should make the other side bat again the following day and how he would have the evening to think about it. Brian turned to Bailey and asked innocently, 'Have you ever slept on it overnight, Trevor?'

There was a collective gasp from the rest of the commentary box followed by silence on the air as Brian struggled to.control himself. Trevor had to step into the breach and for the next three minutes he talked about the weather, the pitch and anything else he could think of, until the others were able to speak.

Daniel Norcross:

It is 2015 and England's women are taking on New Zealand at Mount Maunganui, in North Island. There are no TV cameras, only a couple of members of the press, and the BBC *Test Match Special* team consisting of Charles Dagnall, Henry Moeran and Ebony Rainford-Brent. It is around 3 a.m. in the UK and the listening figures are probably quite low. In addition, doing a full 100-over match with only three commentators is genuinely hard work; the team is struggling with jet lag and the game is meandering more slowly than usual.

At the opposite end of the ground from the commentary box is the Dominion Salt Works, out of which enormous freight trains set out every twenty minutes hauling about ten wagons full of timber. Charles Dagnall, who is probably exhausted and searching for colour to enliven the scene, points out one of these massive trains to Ebony.

Now Ebony Rainford-Brent is without doubt one of the most remarkable people I have ever met. She has a lightning-quick intellect, a dynamic and imaginative mind, and is justifiably proud of her affinity with all things modern – Apple watches, programmable fridges, blenders that talk, all that sort of stuff. But she also has a delightful habit of saying whatever is in her head at any moment.

So, on seeing wood, a substance she clearly considers to have no place in the twenty-first century, she stridently declaims, 'Wood? Who uses wood anymore? I mean, Daggers, you try naming me ten uses for wood.'

Daggers, ever the professional and up for the challenge, responds, 'Well, let's see, shall we? I guess there's bats, stumps, bails, advertising hoardings, picket fences, tables, pavilions – and that's just what I can see right in front of my eyes.'

Ebony, to her credit, realised the absurdity of her position, but in true *TMS* tradition, this didn't stop Daggers from turning the screw for the next half an hour or so, as shots were constantly hit out of the middle of the bat, 'which is made of wood', the ball occasionally struck the stumps 'made of wood', and on and on!

Jonathan Agnew:

When Geoffrey Boycott was a regular summariser on *Test Match Special*, I particularly enjoyed digging the bear traps that he obligingly tumbled into time and again. These were even better when the audience had been tipped off.

For example, not many people would bother to compare the run-scoring rates of Geoffrey Boycott and Jonathan Agnew in one-day internationals, but the cricket-mad *Harry Potter* actor Daniel Radcliffe once did, and sent his findings to us by text from New York. These, as I informed the listeners, revealed that, at 66 runs per hundred balls, my average rate of scoring was faster than Geoffrey's 53 per hundred balls. Our listeners love this sort of thing, and knowing that Geoffrey was due to join me at the microphone very shortly, I told them that I would confront him with this information.

I was, however, honest enough to mention that Daniel's statistics were based on my solitary innings in one-day internationals, in which I had scored two runs from three deliveries, while Geoffrey had batted, albeit slowly, thirty-four times for his 1082 runs.

'Welcome back, Geoffrey,' I began when he returned to the box. 'You won't have heard my discussion with Victor just now, but I presume you'd agree with me that a batsman with a strike rate of 66 must be a better player than one whose scoring rate is only 53?'

I could almost feel the nation holding its breath, waiting for Geoffrey Boycott to concede that I must have been a better batsman than he was.

'Well, that's right,' he replied, and I swear I heard a loud cheer from listeners sitting in the crowd outside our commentary box window. 'Mind you,' he continued after a short pause for thought, 'I'd have to see how many times they'd batted to be absolutely sure.'

I tried for a while to argue against that obviously crucial criterion, but Geoffrey was having none of it. So, having secured what I took to be a victory of reasonable significance, I handed over the piece of paper bearing the information, and its source.

'I'll 'ave that bloody little wizard!' Geoffrey shouted, thumping the desk, knowing that he had come within a hair's breadth of months of merciless leg-pulling!

Michael Holding:

The commentator that I have to field the most questions about is dear old David 'Bumble' Lloyd.

'Is he as bonkers as he comes across?' I'm asked.

'Absolutely,' I tell them without hesitation.

Bumble can be serious when he needs to be, although most of the time he is having fun. He can get away with saying things that others cannot. In Australia for the last Ashes tour, he was on particularly good form. He had an oyster fetish on that tour and for some reason he decided to try to eat a thousand of them over the duration of the tour. (Don't ask me why.)

During commentary, someone asked him how his oyster opus was going.

'How many are you up to now?'

Bumble, with a cheeky look on his face, quipped, 'It puts lead in your pencil, you know!'

There was pandemonium in the box when he said that. His co-commentator couldn't speak for the laughter, the rest of us were in a terrible state and Barney Francis, the poor producer, could only manage a faint, 'Bumble, please,' because it was suppressed by snorts. He had an unforgettable look of fear in his eye. He knew there would be more.

Bumble, knowing he had his audience and a co-commentator silenced, delivered the pay-off.

'But with all that lead in your pencil, it's very important to have someone to write to!'

Daniel Norcross:

Ebony Rainford-Brent may have had her leg pulled by Charles Dagnall, but she is perfectly capable of dishing it out as well. We had worked with each other for a few years before we were sent to Bangladesh in 2016 to cover England's Test tour there. She knows that I have a fondness for abstruse and eclectic words and she usually ignores me if I go a little over the top, but at Chittagong she decided enough was enough.

Umpire Kumar Dharmasena was having a shocker on the field of play. Three of his decisions were overturned by DRS within ten minutes of each other and I was chewing my way through the thesaurus in an attempt to describe the horror show that the poor fellow was having. After a lengthy passage of invective, I sighed, paused, and said simply, 'Well, enough of this taradiddle. Let's hope he can put this behind him and get the next decision right, at least.'

Ebony, with an unusually raised eyebrow, shot back, 'Taradiddle?'

'Yes,' I said, 'it's one of my favourite words. Look it up.'

I then returned to the action on the field, called a

couple of balls, and thought no more about it, until with perfect timing at the end of the over, Ebony came in with: 'Taradiddle, *noun* – pretentious nonsense.'

I had no comeback to that!

Bill Frindall:

Trevor Bailey could be splendidly vague and absent-minded at times. On the rest day of his debut Test in 1949 against New Zealand at Headingley, he took his wife on an unsuccessful trip to find the seaside at the spa town of Harrogate. On one memorable occasion, he entered the commentary box, rubbed his hands with glee and announced that he had just bought a new car.

'What did you buy?' I asked.

He replied, 'I'm not sure. It's a blue one!'

Barry Johnston:

Johnners often used to call Fred Trueman 'Sir Frederick', although he was never awarded a knighthood, much to his disgruntlement! In the early 1980s, Brian wrote a new book and he asked his publisher to send a copy to all the members of the *Test Match Special* team. He wrote something inside each one, and in Trueman's he wrote:

To Sir Frederick, with happy memories
of days in the commentary box.

He thought no more about it until Peter Baxter told him later what had happened. One morning Fred's postman ran up to his front door shouting, 'You've got it at last, Fred!'

When Fred opened the door, there was a parcel addressed to *Sir* Frederick Trueman. Fred hurriedly tore the paper from the parcel only to discover that it had not come from 10 Downing Street or Buckingham Palace, but was a copy of Brian's book. The secretary at Brian's publishers had read what he had written inside and addressed the parcel accordingly.

What Fred said when he found out the truth is not repeatable in polite company!

Daniel Norcross:

At The Oval in 2021 for the England v India clash, I found myself on commentary with Phil Tufnell. He is one of my favourite summarisers. His passion and enthusiasm for the game is unmatched, and he has a very keen eye for what is happening on the field of play. His knowledge is worn lightly, and his playful wit makes every day alongside him in the box a genuine joy. But he does have a very gullible streak, which was exposed on the last day of the match.

Knowing that I wasn't covering the fifth and final Test, and so we wouldn't see each other until the season was over, he asked me where and when my season was going to end. Now, the 2021 summer was pretty arduous. With the launch of the Hundred as well as eight men's Test matches, numerous ODIs, and two series for the women, we'd had a fairly hectic time of it, and it is 'traditional' to let your hair down somewhat after the last game you cover.

So when I told him my last match would be at Canterbury in late September, he gave me a very sympathetic, 'Aw, mate, I'm sorry.'

'Sorry about what?' I asked.

'Well, Canterbury. No one wants the last game to be at Canterbury. I mean, there are no night clubs and all the pubs shut early.'

'Do they?' I queried.

'Yes. It's all to do with the Archbishop of Canterbury. He won't let boozers stay open into the night.'

'I can't think that's true, Tuffers,' I said. 'I mean, there's a university there for a start.'

'Well, that's what my skipper always told me when Middlesex went to Canterbury. I just sat out those games in my hotel, as there was nothing to do.'

Now that is what I call inspired captaincy. Hats off to his skipper Mike Gatting. I haven't double-checked, but I wouldn't be surprised if Tuffers' figures at Canterbury are better than anywhere else he's played!

David Gower:

Ian Botham has a natural and overriding sympathy for the player, as we saw when he spoke up in support of Andrew Flintoff after the infamous 'pedalo' incident at the 2007 World Cup in the West Indies [*when an inebriated Flintoff had to be rescued from the sea after capsizing on a pedalo in the middle of the night*].

I was in our beachside studio in Barbados talking to Athers in St Lucia with Beefy alongside him. Beefy had just got out of bed and been confronted with the issue, and details of what had gone on the night before were in any case still emerging.

There were suggestions that some supporters had 'shopped' Flintoff to the papers, and Beefy said, 'Well, what I want to know is, what were those supporters doing up at 3 a.m.?'

'Er, but Ian, they're not playing for England,' I replied. 'It doesn't really matter what *they* were doing up at that time of night!'

'Well, yes . . . ,' he said, 'I suppose . . . !'

Henry Blofeld:

Ollie Milburn was used on several occasions as a summariser on *Test Match Special* and he made some telling contributions. He will probably be remembered longest, however, for an unfortunate gaffe during a Test at Headingley. He was asked to be in the commentary box at about eight o'clock one morning to do the early breakfast-time programmes.

When the time came, they were unable to raise him at the ground and so they checked at the hotel. Sure enough, Milburn had overslept, but he was told that it would be fine and he could do the programme on the telephone from his room, making it sound as if he was at the ground. The interview started promisingly. Then, halfway through, the interviewer suddenly asked him what the weather was like.

'I don't know,' came the reply. 'I haven't opened the curtains yet!'

Brian Johnston:

One of the great things for me is the number of letters we get from young boys and girls, which is good, because I know how difficult it is nowadays for cricket in schools.

Sometimes the letters are technical. They want to know about laws, or about cricketers, and we had a wonderful one a few years ago.

Fred Trueman had been going on all afternoon, saying, 'Johnners, cricket is a sideways game. Get the left shoulder over the elbow, a straight bat – sideways on. When you're bowling – sideways – get the swivel action, look over your left shoulder. It's a sideways game, Johnners, a sideways game.'

He went on like this and he was quite right. It *is* a sideways game. About four days later, we got a letter from a young boy, who wrote: 'Dear Mr Trueman, I was listening to you the other day about cricket being a sideways game. I'm afraid it hasn't worked with me. I'm a wicketkeeper and I let eighteen byes in the first over!'

The other thing they do is send me stupid riddles: 'Ask Fred what animal he would like to be if he was standing naked in a snow storm.'

'I don't know, Johnners. What animal would I like to be?'

'The answer is: a little 'otter!'

They send in terrible jokes: 'What's a Frenchman called if he's shot out of a cannon?'

'I don't know, Johnners.'

'Napoleon Blownapart!'

'Who was the ice-cream man in the Bible, Fred?'

'No idea.'

'Walls of Jericho!'

Daniel Norcross:

The *Test Match Special* wind-up is a tradition as old as the programme, but perhaps the most elaborate and brilliantly constructed hoax was perpetrated on Geoffrey Boycott at The Oval in 2017. Geoffrey famously made his 100th hundred in an Ashes Test match at Headingley in 1977, and as a man who is seldom shy of his achievements, he was celebrating its fortieth anniversary with a lunch for 180 people in aid of the Yorkshire Air Ambulance.

Jonathan Agnew spotted the perfect opportunity for a wind-up and enlisted the help of Henry Moeran, who at that time was the assistant producer on the programme, and the legendary scorer Andrew Samson. None of the rest of the commentators, of which I was one on that day, were told anything to ensure there was no possibility of a leak. This was proper cloak-and-dagger, secret agent territory.

Aggers constructed a perfectly worded statement from

the ICC, which Henry mocked up on ICC-headed note-paper. Even to the trained eye, this looked authentic. Then they waited for Geoffrey to begin his stint in the commentary box. Aggers, cool as a cucumber, then told Geoffrey what this official statement contained. Apparently, the ICC had deemed the England v Rest of the World matches in 1970, which replaced an originally planned tour by the ostracised South African team, were no longer to be first-class matches.

Geoffrey was initially unperturbed until Samson explained the ramifications. Geoffrey had scored a hundred against that team, had he not?

'Yes, it was here at The Oval, but so what?'

'Well, what I think Aggers is driving at,' said Samson in a matter-of-fact tone, 'is that your hundred at Headingley is no longer your 100th, but instead is your 99th.'

Geoffrey was furious. 'It's ridiculous! It's just politics. Absolute nonsense!'

Samson and Aggers agreed that it was nonsense, but surely his anniversary lunch would now have to be cancelled and all the commemorative plates that Geoffrey had had made up would have to be destroyed.

'So where *was* his 100th hundred?' asked Aggers.

'That would have been against United Bank Limited in Faisalabad on the tour of Pakistan,' replied Samson. 'Not quite the same as an Ashes Test at Headingley, eh, Geoffrey?'

By now Boycott was distraught. 'It's just rubbish. Rubbish, I tell you!'

Then Aggers stood up. It was the end of the over and time for a change in the commentary box. 'Yes, it is rubbish, Geoffrey. It's all been a wind-up.'

'You muppet! You absolute muppet, Agnew!' cried Geoffrey. In fairness to the great man, he knew he'd been stitched up like a kipper and took it with great grace, but my word he was worried for a moment.

And you know, none of it would have been possible if England had taken a wicket during that ten-minute segment, as Aggers would have had to abandon the wind-up and focus on the match; so we have Stuart Broad, Jimmy Anderson, and some stout South African defence to thank for producing a moment of pure *TMS* gold!

WEST INDIES

Michael Holding:

If playing for Jamaica was a learning curve, then the curve would have been in the shape of a smile. I seemed to spend most of my time laughing. All the players were great personalities, in particular Renford Pinnock, whom we called Pinny. He was a born joker. Once during a game when it started to rain, he walked on to the wicket and pretended to cover it by laying his handkerchief on the pitch and then disappearing to the pavilion. He had an answer to everything and could have us roaring with laughter in the most tense situation.

One of those was the final trial match played that year at Sabina Park for selection for a Jamaica side to play in the Shell Shield, the big domestic competition in the Caribbean. The selectors would watch the game from the pavilion and on the last day, having made up their minds, they would put the names of the chosen few on the scoreboard. The result was players not concentrating on the game, constantly straining their necks to look at the scoreboard rather than the ball. And if you were in the dressing room, you certainly weren't watching the action, instead nervously eyeing that board while chewing fingernails down to the bone.

The team I was on was batting and everyone was edgy. Enter Pinny, who pointed to the scoreboard and said sarcastically, 'If they don't give me a game, I'm not playin'!'

With that one joke he relaxed us all as we fell about laughing.

Pinny took things slightly more seriously when batting, but in the field he thought he was a stand-up comic. When he was at fine leg for Jamaica in a game against the Australians, he appealed for a leg before when Greg Chappell was struck on the pads. He was the only fielder to do so, because it was going a long way down the leg side. Chappell gave him a look as if he had lost his mind and even the umpire was a bit shocked.

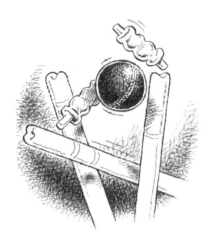

At the end of the over when Pinny was changing field positions, the umpire enquired, 'What are you doing, Pinny? You couldn't possibly see if it was out from down there.'

'That was why I appealed,' replied Pinny. 'I couldn't see whether it was out or not, so I had to ask!'

Fred Trueman:

We claim in England that our umpires are the best in the world, because the majority are former players – and I think that's right. They know the game from the inside and they can be relied upon to understand the problems.

It is a different matter in overseas countries, particularly in the West Indies and (usually for quite different reasons) Australia. There was an umpire called Kippins officiating on the 1959/60 tour of the West Indies who wouldn't give us a thing, and I remember asking him if one decision hadn't been very close. He replied, 'I couldn't give it because I couldn't see any stumps. He was covering the lot!'

In Trinidad every lbw appeal got the same answer: 'Too high.' Then Brian Statham hit a batsman very low on the pad and straight in front, but the umpire said, 'Not out.'

At the end of the over, Geoff Pullar, keeping his face

straight, asked him, 'I suppose that was going *under* the stumps?'

He was told, 'Yes.'

Dickie Bird:

During their 1966 tour of England, the West Indian officials became fed up with the practical jokes being played by members of their team and decided to put an end to them. Larking about was fine in small doses, but the players had gone too far, and enough was enough. Their manager, Jeffrey Stollmeyer, called all the players together to thrash out the matter in a team meeting.

Fast bowler Charlie Griffith arrived late and so didn't know what on earth they were talking about as he sat down to listen to the debate, but his ears pricked up when he heard Garry Sobers say, 'That's it, then. There has been far too much leg-pulling, and it has got to stop.'

Charlie was most indignant. 'No more leg-pulling?' he exclaimed. 'So how am I going to get any runs? That's the only shot I've got!'

Brian Johnston:

At Port of Spain during Colin Cowdrey's successful MCC tour in 1967, I played a dirty trick on the West Indian commentator Tony Cozier. Rain had stopped play and he had gone across to the press box on the other side of the ground. I stayed in the box to give an occasional up-to-date report on the weather. I saw Tony returning after a time, so as he entered the box I pretended that we were on the air, and that I was broadcasting.

'Well,' I began, 'those were the statistics of the MCC team with their exact batting and bowling figures, plus their ages and dates of their birthdays. Thank you, Bearders. Ah, I see that Tony Cozier has just rejoined us, so I will ask him to give exactly the same details of the whole West Indian side. Tony . . .'

I have rarely seen a greater look of horror on anyone's face. He sat down at the mike and began to stammer, making frantic signals to our scorer to hand him *Wisden* or any other book that would give him the necessary information.

'Well, Brian,' he said, 'I'll try to tell the listeners in a minute, but as I've just seen the pitch perhaps you would like to hear about its state first?'

'No, sorry, Tony,' I said, 'we've just talked about it while you were away. All we want – and straight away please – is the information about the West Indian statistics.'

At this point I couldn't go on any further, he looked so miserable and desperate, so I said, 'Well, if Tony won't give us the details, I suppose we had better return to the studio. So goodbye from us all here.' There was a deathly hush for a few seconds, broken only by Tony Cozier's heavy breathing. Then I said, 'Well done, boys. Very good rehearsal!'

It took Tony about five minutes to recover.

Jonny Bairstow:

My dad, David Bairstow, was part of one particular tour that he described as 'horrendous'. In 1981 he went to the West Indies as England's number-one wicketkeeper, but came back as deputy to Paul Downton. That was the tour, lost 2–0, in which a spectator, who also happened to be a policeman, threatened Geoffrey Boycott with a whitewashed brick. Upset by an lbw decision, Boycs had thrown a glass of water out of the dressing-room window and soaked the man accidentally.

This was also the tour when my dad got to know and appreciate the ex-England and Surrey batsman Ken Barrington, who was the team's assistant manager; so dearly loved as a player's man and everyone's favourite kindly uncle. [*Barrington died from a heart attack during the Third Test.*] When you hear about him, you get the sense of someone who was wonderfully eager about everything, so constantly cheerful on your behalf.

Barrington was christened 'Colonel Malaprop', because malapropisms became his trademark. These included:

'There's a lot of bridges to flow over the water yet.'

'I kipped really well. I slept like a lark.'

'That was a great performance in anyone's cup of tea.'

Barrington also discovered piña coladas in the West Indies, but couldn't get his tongue around the pronunciation of it.

Instead, he ordered my dad a 'Peter Granadas', which confused the barman!

Dickie Bird:

Back in 1963 I played for Leicestershire and I always used to open the batting. We were due to play the tourists, the West Indies, at Grace Road but I was having a terrible time. I couldn't get a run. In fact, I was in the second team.

The Leicestershire selection committee – all thirty-nine of them – sat down to pick the team to play against the West Indies and they decided to bring me back into the team. That was a big mistake for a start, because I was in such terrible form.

That 1963 West Indies team was a great side. They had Rohan Kanhai, Basil Butcher, Seymour Nurse, Frank Worrell, the captain, and Garfield Sobers, the greatest all-round cricketer that I've ever seen. But they also had two great fast bowlers – Wesley Hall and Charlie Griffith.

I thought, oh dear! I'm in terrible form and they've selected me to play against these two. Well, I'll get to the ground early tomorrow morning and have a look where we're playing – see what sort of pitch our groundsman has prepared.

Now I'm always early, wherever I go. I arrived that Saturday at about seven o'clock in the morning and I couldn't get into the ground, all the gates were locked. So I threw my bags over the wall, climbed over and went out to the middle to have a look at the pitch.

When I saw it, I couldn't believe it. The groundsman had left the grass on and I thought, oh no! Two of the world's fastest bowlers and Garfield Sobers as first change – and he could bowl a bit, I can tell you – and I always went in first and took the new ball.

So when the groundsman arrived, I said, 'Hey! Get this grass shaved off, man. Make it as flat as you possibly can.'

He said, 'I'm not going to touch it. I want to see some excitement today!'

I said, 'Tha'll see some excitement if thy don't get this grass off.'

He said, 'I'm not touching it.'

So when our captain, Maurice Hallam, arrived, I said, 'Hey, Maurice, if you win the toss, shove the West Indies in to bat, because I don't fancy going out there and playing against Charlie Griffith and Wes Hall.'

He said, 'No. Neither do I, not on here. I'll shove them in if I win the toss.'

I said, 'Don't forget.'

So the two captains went out, Frankie Worrell and Maurice Hallam. Up went the coin, down it came and, after all I'd told him, Maurice won the toss and decided to bat first. Now that was another big mistake. I thought, well, I've got to go out there and do my best. So I padded up and went out with Maurice Hallam to open the innings for Leicestershire.

In those days we didn't wear helmets and we didn't have big chest protectors or thigh pads. We had nothing like that. My 'thigh pad' was my handkerchief. I just kept thinking, I've got to face them, so I took leg-stump guard from the umpire and prepared for the first ball from Wes Hall.

I watched him marking his run-up out at the Pavilion End and I thought, where's he going? I thought he might be going to move the sightscreen. But he wasn't. He was marking his run-up at the side of it. I looked in front of me and I couldn't see any fielders. I thought, that's funny. Where's his fielders? I looked over my right shoulder and, thirty yards back, he'd got nine slips.

I said, 'Are you playing with us?'

I thought, well, I'll show him. I saw Wesley Hall race in and he had this big gold medallion that was swinging in the breeze as he ran, and I didn't see anything else. I think I pushed forward, I don't know, I may have played back, but I saw nothing.

I looked up and all the West Indies players were running round him and hugging him.

'Well bowled, Wes! Well bowled!'

I'm thinking, well bowled? That's funny. Then I looked down and there were no off and middle stumps. Where did *they* go? I looked over my right shoulder and I could see them many a mile past the wicketkeeper.

And I've often thought, if I'd taken off and middle, I don't think I'd be here today!

Peter Baxter:

Brian Johnston had a very quick wit and a mischievous wit as well. One of my favourite examples of it was in the West Indies on tour, when there was a journalist who had an American girlfriend with him that he was rather keen the rest of the press party didn't meet. He found himself in a long corridor and coming towards him was Brian. He had got the girl on his arm and there was no escape. He had got to introduce her, so he thought he would get it over with quickly.

He said, 'Brian, I don't think you've met Annette. Annette, this is Brian.'

Brian said, 'Oh, every time you said you were going to have a net, I thought you were going to practise cricket!'

Michael Holding:

Renford Pinnock was not the only one in the Jamaican side with a quick wit. Leonard Levy, our off spinner and affectionately known as Uncle Sunny, could have us rolling around, too. In a Shield game in the Leeward Islands against what was then called the Combined Islands, he came up with a good one-liner.

One late evening, approaching close of play, our captain, Maurice Foster, asked Uncle Sunny, who was number eleven, to go in as nightwatchman in order to protect Lawrence Rowe. Rowe was our number three and not long before had debuted for West Indies with a double century and century against New Zealand. The explanation given to Uncle Sunny was that it was getting a bit dark and he didn't want to risk Rowe in poor light.

Like a flash, Uncle Sunny quipped, 'But skipper, if the

world's best batsman can't see it because it's too dark, how am I going to see it?'

Thankfully, we didn't lose a wicket and Uncle Sunny was not required!

Matthew Hayden:

Curtly Ambrose was the best opposition bowler I ever faced – by far. You were always under pressure with him. Mark Waugh once said after a one-day innings, 'Does he ever bowl a bad first over?' but I can extend the compliment a little further. I would ask, 'Did he bowl a bad over . . . ever? A bad ball?' I'm sure he did, but it never seemed that way when you were facing him.

Even in retirement, Curtly never lost that bulletproof aura. In 2003, an Australian press photographer saw him in the crowd on the last morning of a Test match in Antigua. The big fella actually agreed to answer one – just one – question. He was asked, 'How would you bowl today if you were still playing?'

Curtly replied, 'If I was still playing today, the game would have been over yesterday!'

Christopher Martin-Jenkins:

I love the West Indies, which I think is probably the most fun tour of the lot in many ways, or it certainly was when the contests were close and West Indies cricket was on a high. It's a beautiful part of the world and, as a journalist, the great thing about it is that you have finished your work whenever plays ends. In a normal day, not floodlit cricket, play ends about six o'clock or a bit earlier in the West Indies, which is roughly ten or eleven o'clock in the UK, so if you're a newspaper man, nothing that happens after that can get into the paper, so you can relax. Although it is not so easy in the days of online reporting, but that used to be the case.

The first tour I did was as long ago as 1973/74 and it was all fresh and new and extremely exciting, as you can imagine working for the BBC. My wife Judy came out to join me for a couple of weeks in Barbados and she was naturally keen to see the island; so we arranged to hire a Mini Moke, and the rules in Barbados state that you have to get a driving permit to drive a hire car in Barbados, and you have to get it from the police station.

So I went round there shortly after my wife had arrived and asked for this driving permit, but unfortunately she had forgotten her driving licence. The chap behind the desk was pretty blunt, he said, 'Sorry, there's no way. If you haven't got your driving licence, you can't get the driving permit.'

So I was feeling rather disconsolate, because Judy was going to be obliged to watch the cricket, when she had rather wanted to go around and see the island. He then noticed the name on the permit form that I had given him and he said, 'Hold on a moment! Are you the fella that talks about cricket on the radio?'

I said, 'Yes.'

He looked at me thoughtfully.

'What do you think of Lawrence Rowe?'

I replied, 'I think he's an absolutely tremendous player,' which was true, because he had just scored 302 against England that afternoon.

He smiled and said, 'What do you think about Alvin Kallicharran?'

I told him I thought he was a terrific player, too, as he had got about 120 against England that afternoon.

We chatted happily about cricket for the next ten minutes or so, when I remembered that I was supposed to be back for dinner at the local hotel, so I said, 'Well, it was lovely to talk with you, but I really must go.'

'What do you mean go?' he said with a big smile. 'You haven't got your wife's driving permit!'

Dickie Bird:

One match I umpired in the West Indies during 1993 stands out in my memory. It was against Pakistan at the Antiguan Recreation Ground at St John's. During the Pakistan innings I was standing at square leg, keeping a keen eye on the batsmen as they scampered for a quick single, when I felt an excruciating pain right at the base of my spine. I thought I'd been shot. The pain travelled all the way down my leg and I collapsed in agony.

It turned out that Keith Arthurton, one of the hardest throwers in world cricket, had hurled the ball in from a position just behind me and had made a slight error in the missile's intended flight path. The physio dashed on, had a quick look, and ordered, 'Right, Dickie, on your feet, and drop your trousers.'

I looked at him aghast. 'I can't do that. Not in front of all these people.'

'Please yourself,' came the brusque reply. 'But I'm warning you, if you don't let me spray the area, then you're going to end up in even more pain. The bruise will be so bad that you won't be able to walk. You'll have a very serious problem.'

There was, it seemed, nothing else for it. So I reluctantly unfastened my belt and allowed my trousers to fall to my ankles, revealing brightly coloured underpants in all their glory.

'Right-oh, then,' I told him, 'get on with it.'

And in my most ministerial fashion, I added, 'Let us spray!'

Vic Marks:

On England's 1990 tour of the West Indies, the facilities in Georgetown, Guyana, were basic and unreliable. It was practically impossible to get a telephone line to the UK, which is the lifeblood of any journalist.

A working telephone was a prized possession on tour and it always seemed to be the case that when Allan Lamb wanted to borrow one to make a social call, he would magically get a line, but when Peter Johnson, the cricket correspondent of the *Daily Mail*, needed a vital conversation with his office, the line was always dead. Peter would dial and dial and nothing would happen. Then, after days of frustration in Georgetown, Johnson eventually got through to his sports desk.

'Peter Johnson,' he said with relief, whereupon the young tyro at the other end paused to check something with a colleague, before blurting, 'No, he's not here; he's in the Caribbean at the moment.'

And slammed the phone down!

Barry Johnston:

On the Australian tour of the West Indies in 1984, their flamboyant batsman Dean Jones wandered on to the beach one day and saw his team-mates having fielding practice, but in a most unusual way – they were standing neck deep in the sea, throwing the ball to one another. The Australian team has always come up with innovative methods of practice and Jones was an enthusiastic fielder, so he decided to join in.

Ever the showman, Dean Jones didn't simply walk into the sea, he broke into a sprint along the beach and performed a spectacular dive into the waves – only to land face down on the sand covered by about a foot of water.

His team-mates burst out laughing. They had set him up by kneeling in the sea to make it look like the water level was higher than it was. Not surprisingly, Jones ended up with a very sore neck. His recovery was not helped by his team-mates frequently calling out, 'Hey Deano!' and getting the giggles every time he turned towards them, causing further painful twinges to his already stiff neck.

CLUB CRICKET

Brian Johnston:

I wasn't a bad wicketkeeper and I wasn't a good one. I was just so-so in club cricket, but I loved it and I played an awful lot. After the war, when I joined the BBC, I was so lucky because there was no Sunday League or whatever it's called now. So you could get all the Test players, and all the visiting teams, to play charity matches on a Sunday.

I kept wicket for fifteen years after the war to all the great bowlers – Lindwall, Laker, Lock, Trueman, Miller, Bedser – you think of anyone, I kept wicket to them. Great fun for me, not much fun for them!

They were very kind to me, but I came down to earth with a bump. I began to think I was getting rather good, playing in these matches, and we went to the Dragon School at Oxford where Richie Benaud, the Australian captain, was playing and I was keeping wicket. He was bowling his flipper and his googly and his top spinner and his leg break. I was reading them all well . . . they all went for four byes, but I read them well!

Then the last chap came in and Richie bowled him a tremendous leg break. This chap went right down the pitch, missed the ball, and it came into my gloves. With all my old speed, so I thought, I flicked off the bails, just like that, and the umpire said, 'Out!'

It was a great moment for me, a club cricketer, stumping someone off the Australian captain. So I was looking a bit pleased with myself when I walked off the field and the bursar of the school came up and said, 'Jolly well stumped.'

'Thanks very much,' I said.

'Yes,' he went on, 'I'd also like to congratulate you on the sporting way you tried to give him time to get back!'

Michael Parkinson:

I used to play cricket with a man called Billy Hopkinson, who made John McEnroe look like the best-behaved athlete in the world. Whenever he was given out lbw his team-mates would evacuate the dressing room, taking all their gear with them, before Billy returned to vent his rage on whatever he could lay his hands on. The main sufferers were the unfortunate batsmen who were at the crease immediately after Billy was given out.

All they could do was stand and watch as their gear came through the dressing-room window to be followed by Billy's gear, the wooden benches, the matting carpet and, on very bad days, the large brown teapot that the tea ladies borrowed from the church hall, which was only used for funerals and cricket matches.

As befitted a world-class tantrum-thrower, in the field Billy Hopkinson could produce an outburst at the correct tactical time. He was the best 'ooher' and 'aaher' I ever played with and also the best running commentator.

On arriving at the wicket, the new batsman would find Billy staring thoughtfully at a spot just short of a length. 'Looks nasty to me that does,' he'd say, sometimes going down on his hands and knees to calculate the size of an imaginary ridge.

'I've never fancied this wicket since our Albert got his nose broke. Made a right mess it did. You could hear the crack a mile away. Off a slow bowler, too,' he would say, while the batsman tried to look cool.

From that point on, the batsman's survival depended on his ability to concentrate on his game while being subjected to a barrage of propaganda from Billy at first slip. Any ball that went past the bat would bring an anguished 'ooooh' or 'aaaah' from Billy. It didn't matter if it was a yard outside the off stump, Billy reacted as if it had passed though the wickets.

Not surprisingly, Billy wasn't the most popular cricketer in the district. There were many players who disliked being bowled out while in the middle of an argument with Billy about whether or not the previous ball had shaved the wickets.

One player dismissed in such a manner decided on swift justice. Instead of returning to the pavilion he set off after Billy waving his bat like a club. But Billy was soon three fields away and wisely he took no further part in the game, spending the afternoon at home and sending his missus down to the ground for his kit.

I only saw him beaten at his own game once and that was by a dark, squat little man who answered everything Billy said about him with a tiny smile, a neat bow of the head and a 'thank you very much'. Finally, Billy could endure it no longer. At the end of the over he confronted the batsman.

'Aye oop, mister. I've been talking to thee all afternoon and tha's said nowt. What's up?'

The batsman looked at him, smiled, bowed and said, 'Thank you very much.'

Billy turned in despair to the other batsman. 'What the bloody hell's up wi' thi' mate?' he demanded.

'Didn't tha' know, Billy? He doesn't speak English. He's Polish,' the batsman said.

'Polish!' said Billy. 'Polish! What's a bloody Polisher doing playing cricket?'

He was silent for the rest of the afternoon, only occasionally muttering the odd obscenity about foreigners. It never occurred to him that there was something very odd about a Pole who spoke no English and yet played cricket well. He was too busy fuming to consider that he might have been conned by a superior foe.

None of us dared put the point to him and indeed we were glad we hadn't, for otherwise we would have missed those marvellous moments in subsequent matches when, giving a new batsman the ritual spiel, he would look at him and say, 'I suppose tha' speaks English, lad?'

Barry Johnston:

Johnners loved playing cricket but he could never take it seriously for too long. George Thorne probably bowled more balls to Brian than anyone else during their school-days at Eton. According to Thorne, Brian was usually worth two extra wickets to him because he would pretend to encourage the batsmen from behind the stumps. 'Don't worry,' Brian would reassure an incoming batsman, 'Thorne's no good. He'll never get you out!' The batsman would relax, and a few balls later he would be clean bowled.

When batting, because of his speed as a runner, Brian would always go for a quick single and his fellow batsmen had to be on their toes. If a ball was going to the left hand of a right-handed fielder, Brian would often shout, 'Come five!' which so confused the fielder that he would return the ball wildly and Brian would get overthrows.

On one occasion, Brian was batting with the Earl of Hopetoun at the other end, a boy who was slightly over-weight and not very fit. Brian hit a ball towards the boundary and yelled at his partner to run. By the time Hopetoun was turning to start his second run Brian had already completed two and they ran down the wicket together. Brian soon left him behind and by the time he had run four poor Hopetoun was still only halfway through his third. By now the whole field was helpless with laughter and when the ball was finally thrown in to the bowler's end no one could decide which batsman was out.

Thorne says there was never a dull moment when Brian was playing. In 1931 during their first year at Oxford, the two of them played together in an Eton Ramblers match against Windsor House Park, who were mainly cricket-playing Eton masters. Thorne took six wickets in quick succession, all of them clean bowled. After the fourth wicket Brian called out, 'Can't you think of anything else to do? It's hard work picking up these stumps!'

Matthew Engel (from Wisden Cricketers' Almanack 1998):

In Lincolnshire, a friendly between Bardney and Horncastle in 1997 was halted by a hang-glider which crashed into Horncastle fielder John Hague as he was running in to field a ball on the boundary. Hague received a glancing blow on the head.

'I nearly didn't play because I'd woken up with a migraine,' said Hague. 'Being biffed on the head by a hang-glider was all I needed.'

The pilot said he had been trying to avoid a field of crops. The players helped him remove his broken glider before all of them, including Hague, carried on.

The *Horncastle News* headlined the item: 'Bad Flight Stopped Play'!

Christopher Martin-Jenkins:

It takes all sorts to make cricket matches. Jim Swanton, my first journalistic mentor, went on playing to a great age and his final match for his own club, the Arabs, was at Torry Hill against the Band of Brothers, a famous Kent club side, and it was played on a not very good pitch. There were some pretty good cricketers playing against the Arabs, including the opening bowler, and unfortunately the first ball of the match lifted off a length and hit the opening batsman in the eye, in the days before helmets.

He was quite badly hurt, poor chap. He fell pole-axed to the ground, blood pouring from the wound and Jim summoned his wife Ann to come on with the first-aid kit from the Jaguar, which was parked on the edge of the outfield. She came running on to the field with the first-aid kit and as she got to the crease, the stricken batsman just managed to lift his head a little bit from the turf.

Jim Swanton said, 'Oh, I'm awfully sorry. I don't think you've met my wife!'

Dickie Bird:

While speaking at a dinner in Surrey, I heard a lovely story that concerned Berkhamsted CC. One day they were playing Chesham, and the Berkhamsted captain, who had never scored a century in his life, was 98 not out. His team needed 18 to win and there were still a few wickets in hand, with plenty of time left. He found himself with a new partner, a young lad called Jamie Brook, who was making his first appearance for the club. Brook promptly smashed three sixes to win the match, robbing his despairing captain of his long-awaited century. The youngster was dropped for the next match and never played for the team again!

Brian Johnston:

A batsman was playing in a very important match when he saw a funeral passing the cricket ground and he held up his hand to stop the bowler from bowling. Then he removed his cap and stood at the wicket with his head bowed in silence until the funeral had passed. Afterwards he replaced his cap and continued batting, hitting the next ball for six, clean out of the ground. At the end of the over the wicketkeeper said to him, 'That was a very nice gesture of yours, paying such respect to the funeral procession.'

'Well,' said the batsman, 'I've been married to her for thirty years . . . it was the least I could do!'

Barry Johnston:

The astronomer Sir Patrick Moore, presenter of *The Sky At Night* for more than fifty years, used to enjoy playing cricket for the Lord's Taverners charity teams and for his village team at Selsey in West Sussex. He was a moderately successful bowler, thanks to his 'medium-paced leg breaks with a long, leaping, kangaroo-type action'.

His batting, however, was another story. A firm number eleven bat, in a playing career that extended over half a century he achieved the superb batting average of 0.8 runs an innings. In his best season, in 1948, he scored only one run and that was from a dropped catch. That year he shattered the existing record for the most consecutive ducks when he ran up a magnificent eighteen on the trot.

Moore put this remarkable feat down to having only two strokes, 'a cow shot to leg' and 'a desperate forward swat', which he used in strict rotation. Perhaps more importantly, although the astronomer normally sported a monocle in his right eye, he did not wear spectacles when batting. Moore once observed, 'Someone said it wouldn't make any difference if I wore binoculars!'

Harry Thompson: Penguins Stopped Play

The whole Captain Scott obsession was down, in the first place, to Robert. Marcus, an old school friend whom I'd known since I was ten, had arrived at Oxford University at the same time as me, and had fetched up on a landing in Worcester College with two other first-years, Terence and Robert.

Marcus and I had not been allowed to play cricket by our colleges. Robert was good enough for his college, but couldn't be arsed to get up early enough for the practice sessions. Terence – well, Terence couldn't play cricket either, but he'd happily tag along with the rest of us if we felt like doing something about it. There was only one option open to us. We would start our own cricket team.

We would play fantasy village-green cricket against horny-handed blacksmiths, not spotty, serious-minded student cricket. And we would name our team after Captain Scott, because he came second, and because he did so in the right spirit. We would call it the Captain Scott Invitational XI, because anybody – absolutely *anybody* – could invite themselves to play. It didn't matter if they'd never played before, or if they were complete rubbish – just as long as they did their best.

Our first task was to recruit some more players, which we did by means of a classified ad. None of the motley bunch that assembled in my college room that wintry night had ever played the game before, except Tom Cairns, a would-be actor in impossibly tight leather trousers, who assured us that he was a rather nifty bowler. Now, when somebody tells you that they're rather good at any sport, it means they're either (a) a five times Olympic gold medallist or (b) utterly useless. We took Cairns at face value – none of us had ever seen trousers that tight before – and it was only when his bowling average sailed past the 100 mark in mid-season that we realised he too was a member of the latter category.

Our first game, against the village of Bladon, north of Oxford, could not have conformed to the pictured idyll more closely: a blazing mid-May day of the kind that comes around once every hundred years or so, a gorgeous wooden-railed pitch at the bottom of a hill beneath the stately bulk of Blenheim Palace, sheep grazing along the boundary, a pond glittering between the trees, and an opposition composed entirely of gnarled Mummerset yokels. One of our players asked for ice in the pub.

'Oice? For the Captain Scott XI? Har! Har! Har!' The entire pub rocked with laughter.

'No, I really would like some ice,' he explained, where-upon the pub fell about again, a procedure that was to be repeated several times before he retreated in disarray.

It was only when the game began that it finally dawned on us that we didn't have the slightest idea what we were doing. I made the deeply humiliating personal discovery that my own cricketing ability roughly approximated to that of Mother Teresa of Calcutta. I couldn't bat, bowl or field, let alone captain. Batting, for instance, bore no resemblance whatsoever to the childishly easy activity portrayed on television. If you've never tried it, imagine trying to hit a swerving cherry tomato travelling at 100 mph, wielding a broom handle.

After Bladon had declared on a comfortable 250 for 4 (a huge score for a village match, had we but known it), we proceeded serenely enough to 58, courtesy of Robert and

Tom Cairns, who could bat a bit even if he couldn't bowl. Thereafter Robert was given out lbw by Terence (incorrectly, as it turned out, for he hadn't read the rules) and the whole thing fell to pieces. Robert chased Terence into the trees with a cricket stump. The next eight men scored five runs between them. Five of us made 0. I did indeed manage to whack my first ball for miles and miles. Unfortunately, I did so vertically, and was caught when it finally returned earthward, having disturbed several Russian satellites. We were all out for 63, and lost by 187 runs.

And so the new-born Captain Scott XI went about its business. We quickly became known as the worst team in Oxfordshire, utterly inept in every department. In one match we were all out for 7, in another for 8. I hit every ball I received vertically upward, and by the end of the season had mustered the princely total of one run. My only consolation was that Marcus had accumulated 0. Even our wicketkeeping – this was Robert's job – was a hopeless mess, because Robert refused to collect any ball travelling down the leg side of the wicket, lest the need to scurry across compromised his dignity. Such leg byes frequently accounted for a quarter of the opposition total, usually more than our whole team had managed between them.

Robert was discreetly replaced behind the stumps by Terence, who was no better; indeed, Lot's wife would have been more agile. Terence did, however, afford us all some amusement when he took a particularly fast delivery in the testicles, after which it was discovered that he had not been wearing a box. Once he had finished writhing around in agony he was offered one, but declined, as there was only one ball left in the innings, and such a thing was hardly likely to happen twice in two balls.

You've guessed it. That is, of course, precisely what happened next. The first time, he had received some rudimentary medical attention. The second time, he was left to roll around in agony by himself, as the rest of us were rolling around alongside him, helpless with laughter.

Christopher Martin-Jenkins:

There's only one snag really with being a cricket journalist and commentator and that is there is too little time actually to play cricket, which is the most fun of all. However, I did manage to play quite a bit of cricket over the years. I've been a member of MCC since 1967 as a playing member. You had to play qualifying matches and one of my first was at a time when Keith Boyce, the Barbados and West Indies fast bowler, was qualifying for Essex. It was in 1966.

Boyce had already cut a swathe earlier in the season through local club sides and his reputation had grown. The MCC captain won the toss and chose to bat, which was the customary thing to do, and he came back into the dressing room and he said, 'Has anyone of you ever stopped a hat-trick?'

I said, 'Well, yes. As a matter of fact I did, last season.' I had gone in and managed to keep the third ball out.

He said, 'Right. You're batting number four!'

Barry Johnston:

During a match between St Peters and Horsted Keynes in May 1999, Sussex dentist Rob Hemingway sent an impressive six soaring over the boundary rope and into the car park, but the smile froze on his face when he heard the distinctive tinkle of broken glass. Hemingway had become the first batsman of the season to hit a six through his own car windscreen.

'It was quite nice to connect with the ball so early in the season,' said the unlucky dentist later, 'but then I heard the crack and thought, oops, whose car is that?'

Brian Johnston:

Harold Larwood was once staying with a friend in the West Country, and visited a village cricket match on the Saturday afternoon. The visiting side were one short and Larwood was pressed to play without anyone knowing who he was. As both umpires came from the home side, who were batting, it proved difficult to get them out.

In desperation, the captain asked Larwood if he could bowl. He said that he would have a try and, taking a short run, sent down an off-spinner, which the batsman missed. It hit him in the middle of both legs, which were right in front of the wicket. Larwood appealed and 'Not out' was the reply. The next one, a leg break, was snicked into the wicketkeeper's hands. Again 'Not out' was the reply.

Larwood then took his usual run of over twenty yards and sent down a thunderbolt, which knocked all three stumps out of the ground. Turning to the umpire he said, 'We very nearly had him that time, didn't we?'

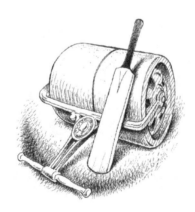

BOWLERS

Dickie Bird:

I would like to have seen Harold Larwood and Bill Voce bowl. They both played for Nottinghamshire and England and I'm told they were very, very quick. One time they were playing Northamptonshire at Northampton and in those days they had a fast bowler in the Northampton-shire side called Nobby Clark. He was very fast. He was left-arm over the wicket and he was letting the Notting-hamshire batsmen have everything – bouncers, beamers, the lot. They were ducking all over the place. The Northamptonshire lads said, 'Hey, Nobby, don't you think you ought to bowl them a few half-volleys? We've got to go in to bat and they've got Larwood and Voce, two of the world's fastest bowlers.'

'What're you frightened of?' said Nobby. 'I'm not frightened of Larwood and Voce. When I come in to bat, if Larwood pitches it in my half I shall hit him straight back over his head. If Larwood bowls short, I'll hook him straight out of Northampton. What're you fright-ened of?'

Nobby had got seven wickets and Larwood came in at number nine. The first ball to Larwood, Nobby let him have a vicious bouncer, straight at his head. Larwood just got out of the way of it. He said, 'Nobby, it will soon be my turn.'

Nobby said, 'Yes, and I shall be ready for you. When I come in to bat for Northamptonshire, you pitch them in my half, Lol, and I'm going to hit you straight back over your head. You bowl them short and I'm going to hook you straight out of Northampton.'

Larwood said, 'It will be a good contest.'

Northamptonshire went in to bat and they tell me they've never seen bowling as quick as they saw that day from Larwood and Voce. They just ran through them, and Nobby came out to bat at number nine. As he was taking guard off the umpire, Lol Larwood said, 'Now then, Nobby, it's *my* turn.'

Nobby said, 'Yes, and I'm ready for you. You pitch them in my half, I'm going to hit you straight back over your head. You bowl them short and I'm going to hook you straight out of Northampton.'

Larwood said, 'We'll see about that.'

In came Larwood, first ball to Nobby, and he bowled him a vicious bouncer, straight at Nobby's head. Nobby didn't just sway out of the way of it, he jumped out of the way, and as the ball went past he flashed at it. Nobby got a thick edge and the ball flew to third slip, who caught it *after* it had bounced two yards in front of him.

Everybody looked up. Nobby, bat under his arm, gloves off, was walking back to the pavilion.

'Come back and fight!' said Larwood. 'Come back and fight!'

'Oh, well bowled, Lol,' said Nobby. 'Well bowled.'

The umpire said, 'Come back, Mr Clark! He didn't catch it. It bounced two yards in front of third slip before he caught it.'

But Nobby kept on walking. He said, 'I am satisfied it was a fair catch, Mr Umpire . . . !'

Andrew Strauss:

Darren Gough was the life and soul of the England team for more than a decade and after a couple of days in his company it was easy to see why. He has an enormous amount of confidence in his ability and he never appears to let things get him down. England might be struggling and Gough may have been smashed around the park, yet he is still full of optimism and enthusiasm. One famous Gough story comes from the 1998/99 tour of Australia when England's bowlers were getting hit all around the Bellerive Oval in Hobart.

The game was in mid-December and Gough, who was not playing in the match, thought it would be funny to come in at the tea interval dressed as Santa Claus and hand out presents. The dressing room would have been a pretty glum place as Gough walked in and everyone was wondering what he would do next.

He chuckled, 'Ho! Ho! Ho! Gussy and Corky. No wonder this bag feels so heavy – it's got your bowling figures in it!'

The batsmen rolled about the dressing room in laughter. The bowlers wanted to strangle him.

Dickie Bird:

During the days of Wilfred Rhodes, one of the greatest all-round cricketers the world has ever seen, Yorkshire paid a visit to Cambridge University and the Yorkshire and England legend was bowling to a young University freshman. To the amazement of everyone, the batsman proceeded to knock Rhodes all over the field and went in at lunch on 99 not out.

While they were having lunch, one of the Cambridge players said to the batsman, 'I can't believe what you've just done. You do know, don't you, who it is that you've just been thrashing around Fenners?'

The young man replied, 'No, I've no idea. Who is it?'

'That,' said his team-mate, 'just happens to be the great Wilfred Rhodes.'

The batsman was still reeling from that piece of information when he resumed his innings at the start of the afternoon session, needing just one more for his century. Now knowing who the bowler was, he was a bag of nerves – and was out first ball!

Barry Johnston:

During the 2001 Ashes series, the young Leicestershire bowler James Ormond came out to bat in the Fifth Test at The Oval. Australia had declared their first innings on 641 for 4 and Ormond, making his Test debut at the age of twenty-four, had taken just one wicket for 115 runs. He was greeted by Mark Waugh, younger twin brother of the Australian captain Steve Waugh, with the remark, 'Mate, what are you doing out here? There's no way you're good enough to play for England.'

Ormond retorted, 'Maybe not, but at least I'm the best player in my family!'

Dickie Bird:

The Sussex and England fast bowler John Snow was involved in a memorable prank in a county championship game at Leicester. It was cold and it was raining on and off, although not heavily enough to justify abandoning the game. The spectators gradually drifted away so that eventually the only people left watching were the scorers and officials.

After yet another stoppage, Snow went out to resume his over. He took out of his pocket a bright red soap cricket ball that he had bought at the local Woolworths, and craftily swapped it for the real thing. His first delivery was the perfect bouncer. The soap ball skidded on the damp grass and Peter Marner, the Leicestershire batsman, got into position for a fierce hook, which he completed with impeccable timing. The ball shattered into fragments.

The Sussex scorer, Len Chandler, placed an asterisk beside the dot in his book, and at the bottom of the page, he elaborated briefly, 'Ball exploded!'

Barry Johnston:

Dennis Lillee was bowling to a batsman who kept playing and missing. After a while the Australian fast bowler could stand it no longer. Lillee went up to the batsman and said, 'I know why you're batting so badly.'

Naturally curious, the batsman asked him why.

Lillee replied, 'Because you've got some shit on the end of your bat.'

The batsman picked up his bat and examined the end of it.

'Wrong end, mate,' said Lillee.

Andrew Strauss:

Darren Gough is always great value because of the stupid comments he comes out with. A journalist once asked him why he was nicknamed 'Rhino'.

'It's because I'm as strong as a bloody ox, that's why,' came the no-nonsense reply.

One morning Gough walked into the England dressing room and informed the team that he had found a great new bar in town. It was lively and, apparently, it served excellent food. When asked what it was called, he replied in his best Barnsley/Italian accent, 'Albarone.'

Albarone? The room went quiet. It was only when he explained where the bar was that a colleague politely pointed out the place was actually called 'All Bar One'!

Michael Parkinson:

Cec Pepper spent most of his career in English league cricket, but there was never any doubt about his roots. He was a dinky-di Aussie, a turbulent man and one of the best all-round cricketers Australia has ever produced. Pepper became one of the legendary figures in league cricket in the north of England. He was playing in one match at Burnley when an amateur in the side, Derek Chadwick, ran round the boundary to catch a skier off the Australian's bowling and collided with the sightscreen.

Play was held up while Mr Chadwick was revived, giving Mr Pepper time to mull over what he considered to be a chance missed off his bowling. Some time later, with Burnley struggling, the captain asked Pepper what he should do.

Cec replied, 'Why don't you get that lad to run into the sightscreen again, it might distract the batsmen!'

Dickie Bird:

Merv Hughes was a tremendous character and I always got on well with him. But in a Test match at Headingley, England were playing Australia and Merv was bowling to Graeme Hick. Now Merv didn't rate Graeme Hick at all, he didn't think he could play, and his language was disgraceful. Honestly, Hick was playing and missing and Merv was swearing, with that big walrus moustache of his quivering, and I've never heard language like it.

I said, 'Merv, I want you to be a good boy. I want you to stop swearing.'

He said, 'This fella can't play.'

I said, 'Look, Merv, be a good boy and stop swearing, please. Now go back to your mark and get on with your bowling.'

Merv walked past me to go back to his mark, to bowl the next delivery, and he looked at me as he walked past. He said, 'Dickie, you're a legend!'

I said, 'Well, be a good boy now, no more swearing.'

He said, 'All right, Dickie, for you I'll not swear again.'

And next ball Hick played and missed and you've never heard language like it!

Barry Johnston:

During the 2002/03 Ashes series in Australia, there was some discussion in the international media about the bowling action of the Australian fast bowler Brett Lee, suggesting it might not be entirely legal. At the Fourth Test in Melbourne the English touring supporters, 'The Barmy Army', were in full voice and they lost no opportunity to remind Lee that they considered him to be a chucker. Whenever the young Australian came in to bowl, the English fans would call out, 'No-ball!' causing the Australian batsman Justin Langer to label them 'a disgrace'.

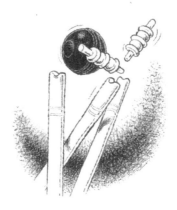

When Brett Lee was not bowling, he fielded directly in front of the English fans and it seems he took their good-natured stick in his stride. At one point he even responded with a smile when the Barmy Army asked him for a wave. The smile was soon wiped off his face, however, when they asked him to repeat the gesture ... but with a straight arm!

Dickie Bird:

Merv Hughes was never short of a word or three. On one occasion Javed Miandad, of Pakistan, found himself out-manoeuvred by Merv during a Test match in which there was considerable needling. Merv had a go at Miandad, who jabbered back nineteen to the dozen, eventually snarling, 'Oh, get back to your mark, you bus conductor.'

Merv bridled. The old moustache started quivering. His nostrils flared. And he stomped back muttering dark curses under his breath. He tore in like a man possessed for the next delivery and clean bowled Miandad. As the Pakistani tucked his bat under his arm and took off his helmet to make his way back to the pavilion, Merv called out, 'Tickets please!'

Ricky Ponting:

Brad Hogg, the 'chinaman' bowler from Western Australia, is a rare individual, razor keen; a man who thrives on putting the team above himself. I can't stress how important blokes like Hoggy are to the psyche of a cricket team on tour. Sometimes their off-field selflessness and good humour can be just as important for a team's progress as a hundred made on the park. Hoggy's other rare skill was his ability to get everyone feeling good without even trying, such as the time we were on the bus to Dambulla, north-east of Colombo, in Sri Lanka. He looked down at his watch and then asked our team manager Steve Bernard how far we had to go.

'Probably another two hours,' Brute replied.

Hoggy stopped for a moment and then inquired, 'So when will we get there?'

Then there was the time immediately after we went 2–1 up in the Test series in Sri Lanka, when he was told by Jock Campbell, our fitness trainer, there wouldn't be a net session the next day.

'No mate,' Hoggy replied. 'I want to bowl twelve balls tomorrow.'

'Why twelve?' asked Jock, who was keen for the bowlers to have a rest.

'Four leg breaks, four wrong'uns and a flipper,' our man answered.

'That's only nine,' Jock said with a look of bewilderment on his face. 'What about the other three?'

Hoggy explained, 'They're spares, in case any of the others don't come out right!'

Michael Atherton:

It was my final Test match. Australia had progressed serenely to 641 for 4 and had enforced the follow-on. On the Sunday evening I had played my last innings and now, as the team went out to prepare for the final day, I stayed in the dressing room at The Oval for treatment. It was almost as if I was physically removing myself now that my contribution was done. I looked upon the match situation, and the problems, dispassionately, from a distance.

I was determined to enjoy my last day, however. Mostly, I watched on television from a corner in the dressing room, trying to commit to memory a place I might never see again.

In the afternoon Graham Thorpe hobbled in. 'I'm sorry to have missed your last game, Athers,' he said, 'but I'm proud to have played with you.' At the end, Duncan Fletcher, the England coach, gave a small speech of thanks for my efforts over the last fifteen years, and urged everyone to come to the dinner in my honour that night. I was getting a little emotional.

I wasn't the only one. Phil Tufnell had taken a mauling in the match. Now he sauntered over with a fag in his mouth and a sad look on his face. I took his limp, outstretched hand and awaited his eulogy.

'Athers,' he said, 'I bowled all right, didn't I? Jesus, I've gone for 170 on a "bunsen" but I bowled well . . . didn't I?'

Michael Parkinson:

When he was in his eighties, the Australian bowling legend Bill 'Tiger' O'Reilly had to have one of his legs amputated below the knee. Neither cruel illness nor old age could change his feisty manner. He was a mettlesome man, full of opinion and argument.

When I called to inquire about his condition, he said, 'I just sit here watching the kitchen wall in case someone runs off with it. It is a very boring occupation, but I have to tell you that it is infinitely more interesting than watching one-day cricket!'

Dickie Bird:

I played with one of the greatest characters at Yorkshire – Fred Trueman. He was also a great fast bowler, although I thought Dennis Lillee of Australia was the best fast bowler I had ever seen, and I used to argue the point with

Fred every time I saw him. He'd say, 'Tha' what? Huh! I can still bowl better now off five paces than he ever could!'

Fred was great fun to be with in the dressing room. We always had a laugh. Before a county championship match started, we'd get changed in the Yorkshire dressing room but Fred was never in our room before the match started. He always went to see the visitors. He didn't knock on the visitors' dressing-room door, he just used to smash it open.

He used to stand in the entrance and he'd say, 'Nah then, lads, I'm here and I'm ready for you today. I can see you shaking a little bit, yes, you're looking a little bit uneasy. I think I might have eight or nine wickets here today. Oh, there's my old friend from last season. He was by the square-leg umpire when I bowled him. That's one wicket I've got for a start! Anyway, good luck, lads. I shall be ready for you in the middle. I can see all of you are looking a bit worried.'

If we'd lost the toss and the visitors were batting, the Yorkshire team would be out in the middle with the two umpires and we'd look around saying, 'Where's Fred?' And Freddie would be standing by the pavilion gates. He used to wait for the opposition opening batsmen, and as they came out through the gates he would say to them, 'Don't close that gate. You won't be long out here!'

Henry Blofeld:

There's a nice story about dear old Alan Ross, who wrote beautifully for the *Observer* on cricket for about twenty or thirty years and was editor of the *London Magazine.*

Alan had his finest hour during a game of cricket at Lord's in 1969. The New Zealand cricket side were over here that year and they had in their ranks a chap called Bob Cunis, who wasn't quite a fast bowler, and wasn't quite a slow bowler, and wasn't quite a medium-pace bowler. Alan wrote this one Sunday in the *Observer* and I have a cutting at home: 'The problem with Cunis is that his bowling is rather like his name. It's neither one thing nor the other!'

Brian Johnston:

There are so many stories about Fred Trueman, but one, which Norman Yardley assured me is true, occurred in about 1949, when Fred was eighteen or so. In those days Yorkshire used to go and play matches against various clubs to get fit for the cricket season. Nowadays, people run ten times round the ground or do press-ups, but in those days they used to play cricket to get fit for cricket, which was good!

They were playing the Yorkshire Gentlemen at Escrick and Fred, very young, virile and tough, bowled very fast bouncers at these poor Yorkshire Gentlemen. Four of them were carried off and went to hospital. They were about 26 for 6 when out of the pavilion came a figure with grey hair, white bristling moustache, I Zingari cap with a button, and a silk shirt buttoned up at the sleeves.

Norman went up to Fred and said, 'Look, this is Brigadier So-and-So, patron of the club. Treat him gently, Fred.' So Fred, who was a generous man, went up to the apprehensive-looking Brigadier and, with a lovely smile, said, 'Don't worry, Brigadier. Don't worry. I'll give you one to get off the mark.'

The Brigadier's face relaxed in a smile, only to freeze with horror as Fred said, 'Aye, and with second I'll pin you against flippin' sightscreen!'

Ian Brayshaw:

When the Australian fast bowler Dennis Lillee was at his peak in the early and middle 1970s, his sheer speed was enough to put a falter in the step of the best batsmen in the world. As the years passed he naturally slowed down a little, but he retained the ability to throw in the occasional scorcher, just to let them know it was still there. Umpire Robin Bailhache tells the story of Lillee toiling away with little help from a pretty flat wicket in the First Test against the West Indies at the Brisbane Cricket Ground in 1979/80.

It was hot, frustrating toil for a bowler of Lillee's type and after a while the champion became a little worn and exasperated. At the end of one over a dejected Lillee stood halfway down the pitch and Bailhache moved to save him the walk back to get his hat. As he handed it over, a rather haggard-looking Lillee said:

'Jeez, it's hard being a fast bowler and I ought to know . . . I used to be one!'

COMMENTATORS

Brian Johnston:

The great thing is we do have fun in the commentary box, and we hope we communicate that fun through the microphone. You can't do this without wonderful people in the box and one of them was the great E.W. 'Jim' Swanton. Jim was a marvellous commentator on both radio and television and a great summariser, on television especially. He also wrote for years for the *Cricketer* and the *Daily Telegraph*.

He used to play the odd round of golf, and his ambition was to be a Second World War golfer – out in thirty-nine, back in forty-five!

On tours, though, he was a bit pompous. He used to stay with Governor Generals and arrive at the ground with a flag on the car! In fact, when he was on *Desert Island Discs*, Roy Plomley said, 'Mr Swanton, how do you think you would cope with being on a desert island?'

Jim said, 'It depends who was the Governor General.'

He's a great talker, and I rang up his wife the other day and said, 'How's Jim?'

She said, 'I haven't spoken to him for about three and a half days.'

'Really,' I said, 'has he been away?'

'No,' she said, 'I didn't like to interrupt!'

Jim was always very keen on the differential between the amateur and the professional. He thought it was a good thing. But I think he carried it a bit far when he refused to drive in the same car as his chauffeur.

Richie Benaud:

There are times when, sitting back in your living-rooms, you might think from the slight rise in tone in the commentator's voice that he is excited or, without you knowing it, it could be that a little glitch has appeared. It might be that a camera has 'gone' just at a crucial moment, something to do with the sound, or someone may have pressed an unusual button somewhere in the world.

It might be to do with the commentator, or it could be something to do with production in the director's van at the ground and, on the rare occasion the latter might occur, I have been known to say softly into the 'lazy' mike, 'Everything all right down there . . . ?'

Just after the England v New Zealand Test at Old Trafford in 1994, we went to Headingley to cover the NatWest match between Yorkshire and Somerset. Due to the rain, the commentators' roster turned into a dog's breakfast with additions, deletions and initials everywhere, and Tony Lewis, as presenter, was doing a brilliant job of providing interviews, detail and all other things necessary when nothing at all is happening on the field.

Coming up to what would have been teatime, I knew that I, in the commentary box, needed to keep an eye on things for Jack Bannister, who was on air in the studio with Tony and Geoff Boycott. But, for some reason, I put my brain into Plan B mode and settled down at the small table, earpiece in my ear listening to the discussion, and started on a sandwich and a cup of tea.

I was able to hear the interesting chat between Tony, Jack and Geoff and see it on the monitor on the table beside me. Suddenly there was a frenzied shout from the van and in my ear because Tony had said, 'And now to Richie Benaud in the commentary box.' Plan B changed to Plan A in an instant. I moved at considerable speed and with mixed success.

I dropped the sandwich on the floor and banged my right knee hard on the side of the chair. With the pain from that, I dropped my binoculars on the chair, and my earpiece, which was connecting me with the shouts from the van, became entangled in the connecting wires. When I joined it all together, I found the plug was out of, instead of in, the sound box.

Eventually, while everyone else was hysterically help-less, I was able to say in a suitably calm voice, with only a slight edge to it, 'Now that you've had time to study the scorecard at your leisure . . . !'

In my ear there came an equally calm Welsh voice, but with a definite hint of laughter about it, as Tony Lewis inquired, 'Everything all right up there . . . ?'

Bill Frindall:

John Arlott was certainly the easiest commentator to work with. He rarely required me to pass him anything except the bowling figures or another bottle. He did startle me once during an Ashes Test but it was after he had lunched well.

He said, 'What I really want to know, Bill, is if England bowl their overs at the same rate as Australia did, and Brearley and Boycott survive the opening spell, and there are not more than ten no-balls in the innings, and assum-ing that my car does 33.8 miles per gallon and my home is 67.3 miles from here, what time does my wife have to put the casserole in?'

Brian Johnston:

Another great character on *Test Match Special* was Don Mosey. He was talking about David Gower at Headingley in 1989 when he said, 'This is David Gower's one hundredth Test match and I'll tell you something. He's reached his one hundredth Test in fewer Test matches than any other player!'

Richie Benaud:

When Channel Four took over from the BBC in 1999 there was no doubt about the change in television coverage. Like the BBC, Channel Four went to horseracing on occasions during the afternoon on a Saturday or holiday, but it was very rare for them to go to a news bulletin, which in the late 1990s had become part of the BBC's standard cricket telecast. The newsreaders were very good, but Tony Lewis had a moment he would like to forget in the handover to one of them, the experienced Moira Stuart.

Tony was one of the best television presenters and commentators with whom I've ever worked. We agreed that a day's commentary was like a day playing Test cricket – one must have energy, a clear mind, a solid performance, concentration and quality throughout the day, always with your brain in gear before moving your lips.

Tony, known by some as 'A.R.', tells against himself the story of when, in the late 1990s, he and Geoff Boycott were on the roof at the Edgbaston ground doing a chat show concerning 'Best Catches' and 'Viewers' Questions and Answers'. Keith Mackenzie was directing and the instructions were that at the end of the session, Tony was to hand back to Moira Stuart at Broadcasting House. The handover had to be perfectly timed.

One problem I could visualise from the commentary box was that the positioning of the monitors on the roof was such that the blazing sunshine was making it close to impossible to see what was on the screen. Tony said later that 'close to impossible' was well short of the mark, it was *totally* impossible. He filled exactly the twenty seconds required, threw to Moira Stuart, in his ear was given the all clear and assumed that to be correct.

Never has the phrase 'assume nothing' been more pertinent because the correct cut-off switch had *not* been pressed in the van, or in London, or possibly both. That was why A.R.'s *'For f**k's sake'* made it to Moira at the news desk and to a few hundred thousand living-rooms around the country, also to the office desk of Jonathan Martin, BBC's Head of Sport.

After lunch A.R. read out a prepared apology and also apologised to the head man of the BBC. He needed a bit of lightening up, which was provided a few hours later when Ian Chappell sent him a message that read simply, 'Congratulations A.R., mate, one-all.'

This was a reminder to the effect that Ian had previously made a similar error, having been told he was 'off-air' when in fact the wrong switch had been pressed and he was still 'on-air'.

It wasn't long before Chappell had taken a 2–1 lead in the 'assume nothing' stakes!

Daniel Norcross:

Henry Moeran is a constant source of amusement in the commentary box. He is hugely quick-witted, always speaks with a smile in his voice, and can reduce a co-commentator to tears of laughter with a perfectly delivered *double entendre*. It was during an IPL match in April 2021 featuring the Delhi Capitals' skipper Rishabh Pant that he produced a corker. I was listening in at home when the ball was smashed back at head height by the West Indian Shimron Hetmyer.

His batting partner, I discovered, had to take swift evasive action as Henry pointed out, 'Pant's down at the non-striker's end!'

I was in fits of giggles at home, as no doubt were many other listeners, but mercifully for once, his summariser Alex Hartley had completely missed it.

Henry was himself subject to a giggle fit when his co-commentator Isabelle Westbury, a splendid commentator and summariser, was describing England veteran Jenny Gunn's fine exploits diving around in the field, when she suddenly announced in her cut-glass, Oxbridge accent: 'Jenny Gunn is reaching balls you don't expect she'd be able to!'

Brian Johnston:

During the Third Test of England's tour of the Caribbean in 1960, the West Indian commentator Roy Lawrence welcomed listeners by saying, 'It's another wonderful day here at Sabina Park . . . the wind shining and the sun blowing gently across the field!'

On England's tour of Australia in 1978/79, another commentator said, 'John Emburey is bowling with three short legs – one of them wearing a helmet!'

And an unknown commentator is reported to have informed his radio audience, 'He was bowled by a ball which he should have left alone!'

Michael Atherton:

On my first day for Channel 4 at Lord's I made sure I sat in the box whenever Richie Benaud was commentating. During the afternoon Michael Slater was on air and was all of a muddle. He wanted to use the past tense of the word 'sneak', but wasn't sure whether it should be 'snuck' or 'sneaked'. He turned to the doyen of commentators, who was eating a sandwich and studying the racing form in his newspaper.

'Hey, Rich,' he whispered, 'can I use the word snuck, or is it sneaked? Whadya think?'

Richie finished his sandwich and then ticked his fancy. Then, in characteristic fashion, he raised an eyebrow and half turned to Slater.

'Michael,' he said, 'quite a few "ucks" spring to mind, but "sn" is not one of them!'

Brian Johnston:

We used to pull Jim Swanton's leg unmercifully. One famous example happened in 1963 during that wonderful Test match against the West Indies at Lord's, when Colin Cowdrey came in at number eleven, his wrist in plaster, two balls to go and six runs to win, and with David Allen at the other end. It was a draw, but it was a great match.

Before it started, Jim and I were doing the television and we were told, 'There's ten thousand people in St Peter's Square, waiting for that white puff of smoke to come out of the Vatican chimney and announce that a new Pope has been elected. If this happens during the Test, we'll leave it immediately and go over to our man in Rome, who'll tell us who the new Pope is.'

So we were waiting for this call to Rome, yapping away, doing the commentary, when out of the corner of my eye I saw that the chimney on the Old Tavern had caught fire. Black smoke was belching out, so we got the cameras on to it and I said, 'There you are. Jim Swanton's been elected Pope!'

Henry Blofeld:

Rex Alston was another great commentator. He died in 1994, at the age of ninety-three, but he was an extraordinary chap. He was a schoolmaster by trade, and they always say about schoolmasters, 'a man among boys, a boy among men'. There was a little bit of that about Rex. He was naive. I don't think he'd ever really visited the fleshpots of life, although that may be unkind. But the most extraordinary thing once happened to him.

Towards the end of his life, in 1985, he came up to a dinner in London. He was staying at the East India and Sports Club, I suppose because he was a sportsman – he certainly wasn't East Indian! – but he was taken ill in the middle of the night and rushed off to the Westminster Hospital. The next morning the matron came in, holding a copy of *The Times*, and said, 'Good morning, Mr Alston, I've come to read you your obituary.' His obituary was in the paper!

John Woodcock, the cricket journalist, had written it – for the elderly, the obituaries are usually written in advance and he'd been asked to do one about Rex, knowing that he was getting on a bit. So Woodcock had written it and sent it in to *The Times*. It was a busy day at the paper and the obituaries editor had seen it and thought, 'Oh dear, poor old Rex.' He'd put it in his out-tray and it appeared in the paper the next day.

I rang up John Woodcock, because we'd had a party for the BBC at the Lord's Banqueting Suite earlier in the week, when Rex had been in absolutely mid-season form, and I said to Johnny, 'It's awfully sad.'

He said, 'Blowers, you're the second person who's rung me this morning. You'll be very surprised to hear who the first caller was!'

When he told me, I asked him, 'What did you say to Rex?'

Johnny said, 'The first thing I said to him was, "Rex, now tell me, *where* exactly are you calling from?"'

Bill Frindall:

Brian Johnston was an enthusiastically active president of the Metro Club for the Blind and his regular plugs for the Primary Club on *Test Match Special* greatly boosted that famous charity's membership. One of Johnners' favourite stories involved his interview with a blind parachutist.

Brian said, 'I am full of admiration for what you do. Incredibly courageous. But how on earth do you know when you are about to land?'

The blind man replied, 'Oh, that's no problem! The lead on the guide dog goes slack!'

Henry Blofeld:

I got on very well with John Arlott, but he wasn't an easy man. He was a legend in his own lunchtime – he had an absolutely unquenchable thirst and he was a prodigious drinker of claret. My definitive Arlott story happened at the first Test match I was lucky enough to commentate on at Lord's.

On the second day of the Lord's Test match in those days, the Director General of the BBC, in his infinite wisdom, always had a private dinner party for the members of *Test Match Special*. Now that was frightfully chuffing and all the rest of it, but actually it was a bloody nuisance, because Broadcasting House was at the other end of London from where I lived, and I had to rush back home and change. It was desperately difficult to get there on time and I just breasted the tape at about 8.27.

I knew it was going to be a bad evening when the Director General was in the act of throwing the keys of the drink cupboard to Trevor Bailey with the words, 'Lock up when there's nothing left!' I don't know how well you know Trevor Bailey, but when I tell you that he didn't go to bed until he was fifty-three, you'll know what I mean!

Anyway, at about two o'clock we were down to warm water and so we legged it home. Being a new boy, I got to Lord's quite early the next morning, at about nine-thirty. If you don't know the Lord's pavilion, you go in the back entrance, and then you go up half a flight of stairs to the first landing, which is the Long Room level. There are these rubberised stairs with pockmarks from cricketers' boots, and it smells like a cross between linseed oil and stale jockstraps, the sort of thing that sets cricketers' noses a-twitching about March and April.

I'd got up to the first landing and was contemplating ascending the next three staircases to the commentary box at the top, when I heard a noise like a broken oak tree behind me. 'Henry, will you give me a hand with these?' and there was the great man, Arlott, sweating profusely, mopping his brow with a red-spotted handkerchief, with two enormous brown briefcases.

I rushed downstairs and said, 'Of course,' and picked one up, which was very heavy. I thought of *Wisden*s and other learned tomes, and I picked up the other, which was almost as heavy, and I thought of more *Wisden*s and more learned tomes. We got back to the Long Room level, when the great man spoke again. 'Henry,' he said, 'before we climb Everest we'll go and pay Maisie a visit.'

The Long Room bar, which is parallel and behind the Long Room, was in those days presided over by a lady of Irish extraction called Maisie. Maisie had nothing much going for her except for one thing – she had pink hair. Now pink hair is quite unusual, but the thing about her hair was that it was never the same two days running. Some days it was shocking pink, other days it was not quite so shocking, and then it was more shocking than you could ever believe. I think this was a fairly modest day and we went into the Long Room bar, which had just opened, and Arlott spoke again.

'Maisie,' he said, 'we'll have two quadruple brandies.'

I said, 'No. No, John, not after last night. I'll have some black coffee.'

'Maisie,' he said, 'we'll still have the two quadruples.'

I kid you not, he had a Force Nine hangover on the Richter scale and it was only by dint of getting both hands together and pulling in opposite directions that he eventually got the drink down; some of it went here and there, but quite a lot of it went in. It steadied him up and, to show off, he picked the next one up rather shakily in his left hand and threw it back, got almost all of it in the right place, and I thought, 'Thank goodness for that, now we can get on with the day's work.' Not a bit of it!

'Maisie,' he said, 'to complete the cure, we'll have a third quadruple,' which came and went with sickening speed. There we were at about twenty minutes to ten and the old boy had downed half a bottle of brandy!

We set off up the three flights of stairs. He went at the double and I staggered behind with these great heavy briefcases and I put them down on the green baize table in the corner of the commentary box. I can remember Johnners was there in his favourite old brown-and-white shoes, Christopher Martin-Jenkins was there and our producer, Peter Baxter – I think they'd been recording a programme.

When I'd put the cases down, Arlott waited for a moment and then advanced upon the table with the sort of smile on his face that I can only think the Duke of Wellington would have worn when he left Waterloo for the last time. It was a little bit self-satisfied, I'm bound to say, and pleased.

He went and opened the first briefcase and took out six bottles of claret. He opened the second briefcase and took out four bottles of claret, one or two glasses, corkscrews and sundry bits and pieces, and then he turned to the box. We were all absolutely open-mouthed and he made the immortal remark, 'Well, with any good fortune, that little lot should see us through until the lunch interval!'

OVERSEAS TOURS

David Lloyd:

After I retired from first-class cricket, I was asked to coach the England Under-19 team on their winter tours. Graham Saville, the former Essex batsman, was the manager, and excellent at the job. He was not a tranquil man to have about the place, though. In fact, he was on blood pressure pills as he tended to get over-excited rather easily.

Early in 1996, the Under-19s were on tour in Zimbabwe and we were staying at the Holiday Inn in Bulawayo. At 6 a.m. one day we were loading up the bus for the drive back to Harare, when the hotel manager made an appearance. He had a complaint. There were some unpaid bills, which is unacceptable on any tour.

'What names are on them?' demanded Graham Saville, with a warning flash of anger.

Without even a hint of a smile, the hotel manager replied, 'Mick Jagger, Cliff Richard and Prince Monolulu!'

Charlie Connelly:

In 1994, *Wisden* reported that an English touring team, the Explorers, had played what was said to be the first formal match in Moscow since the Bolshevik revolution. Their opponents were the MCC: the newly formed Moscow Cricket Club.

Owing to a misunderstanding, the pitch was originally laid out for a croquet match. Broom-handles had to be used in place of stumps, as the man bringing some of the kit was stopped at Heathrow because he had forgotten to get a visa.

When I tracked down one of the Explorers, Mark Rice-Oxley, he confessed, 'I can't quite remember what happened,' but when pressed he recalled that there was cake, tea and a string quartet at the tea interval, and the game was played just off Komsomolsky Prospekt on the southern side of Moscow.

The Moscow side – largely comprised of expats but with at least one Russian and one native of Belarus – scored a semi-respectable 112, but the Explorers emerged from a tight game victorious. Most importantly, according to Rice-Oxley, 'I was out for one, but I did get a hatful of wickets on a track more spiteful than Stalin in his heyday!'

Roger Morgan-Grenville:

Ten golden rules for cricket tours in France:

1. Everyone always says that they will come when the tour is first announced. They do this because they want to leave the door open until the last possible moment, in case they find a way of being allowed to go. In fact, no one is in the team until they have emailed the receipt for their booked flight.

2. If you find yourself wondering for more than five seconds if someone will fit in, they won't.

3. Inevitably, someone will think that a pint in Wetherspoons at 5.45 a.m. is a good thing, not because they remotely want one, but because they think mythology will expect them to have had one. Wetherspoons airport pubs are consequently full of quarter-finished pints.

4. Touring virgins must make a contribution of a bottle of Monkey Shoulder triple malt Scotch whisky. That is their buy-in.

5. The wealth manager always starts a food arms race in any given restaurant, meaning that eleven budget tomato salads suddenly metamorphose into eleven steak tournedos in a rapid and financially suicidal exercise in mutually assured destruction.

6. The kitty has never got enough money in it. Until the last day, when it always has too much. Hence, the treasurer never really enjoys the tour.

7. The designated driver is provided with free drinks for his sacrifice, which is a shame, as the law prevents him from ever taking advantage of this.

8. The locals really couldn't care less about what you are doing. They would be more interested in a lecture on dialectical materialism than in learning not to move behind the bowler's arm. They are beyond help.

9. Like the first cuckoo of spring, what players really think of other players only ever emerges on the final night of a given tour, once the Monkey Shoulder has gone.

10. Whatever they say before the tour, no one *actually* wishes to visit that historic castle, those caves or that nice museum, on the Saturday and Sunday morning. They want to go to a vineyard. Any vineyard. And they want to stay there as long as possible.

Jimmy Anderson:

In the winter of 1999/2000, Graeme Swann went on Nasser Hussain's side's tour of South Africa with a new-look England squad. They were aiming to reboot the national DNA with disciplined and dedicated cricketers. God knows what they saw in Swanny. That tour, by his own admission, was a bit of a disaster for him in terms of the cricket. He was too young (not quite twenty-one) and too much of an upstart.

I think they realised their mistake pretty quickly. Duncan Fletcher, the new coach and looking to really drive home this new disciplinarian ethic, had a (not particularly popular) rule that if you weren't at the bus one minute before leave time, he wouldn't wait for you. That just wasn't Swanny's outlook on life.

On the morning of the Centurion Test, having already inevitably been late once on tour, Swanny was not there at 7.59 a.m. for bus call. The coach left without him. Suddenly aware of how much trouble he was in and in a state of blind panic, he blagged a lift to the ground with the photographers. The driver, not a hundred per cent taken with the first two requests to 'chase that bus', ended up being persuaded to drive down the hard shoulder of the motorway in a bid to do some damage limitation to Swanny's impending disciplining.

As they were racing down the slipstream of the motorway, they reached the traffic, which had come to a total standstill on the way to the ground. On the hard shoulder, meanwhile, in a lane of his own, Swanny was darting past all the static, beeping vehicles. Eventually they passed the England coach. Most people would have kept their head down, got there and got on with it. Swanny took the opportunity to climb down and gleefully double-arm wave to the England team on board. First to Michael Vaughan at the back, who laughed, then to Nasser and Duncan Fletcher at the front, who didn't. The way he describes it, daggers don't even come close. They wanted him dead on the spot.

He was first at the ground.

When the others got there, he was tapping his watch, saying, 'What took you so long, lads?'

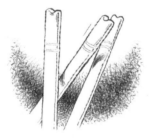

Angus Bell: Batting on the Bosphorus

When I was a whippersnapper I always wanted to play international cricket. I dreamed of steaming in as a tearaway for England and uprooting Brian Lara's off stump. It was a sad day at school when, alas, fully grown at five foot eight, I had to ditch fast bowling and switch to gentle leg spin. I realised I was never going to make it for England. Not deterred entirely, I lowered my sights, setting them on Scotland. It was even more pathetic the day I realised I wasn't going to cut the crust there either. Never in my youth in the Scottish hills, however, did I imagine I'd get my first international cap for Slovakia.

'All our games are internationals,' said Vladimir as we drove to the football field in his red Škoda. 'Tonight it's Slovakia A versus Slovakia B. You can be captain of the A-team, my friend.'

Captain. On debut. Of the A-team. My cheeks flushed and my chest swelled. It was a shame my parents couldn't be here to see this.

I asked Vladimir about the make-up of the squad. Seventy per cent were gardening and/or politics students, he said, and all were native. They also batted left-handed. 'I think this is because of ice hockey.'

But the most startling statistic leapt out from the Slovak team-sheet. Move over the Waugh brothers, Slovakia had four Juricek members, three other sets of brothers and two cousins.

'Their mothers are very proud,' said Vladimir.

The Slovaks arrived by rollerblade, bicycle and moped. Although most of the players had passed their English exams only a week ago, it was a struggle to get anything more than 'hello' out of them.

'These guys,' said Vladimir, pointing at two team-mates, 'recently applied to Nitra University. Everyone must sit entrance exams, unless they are a member of a Slovak national sports team. Nitra University approved their applications based on them playing cricket. But, guess what. They have batting averages of two and zero. One of them has never scored a run in his life!'

The successful applicants giggled and nodded when they understood.

The plastic green pitch was wheeled out to the centre circle. Once Vladimir had broken up a minor scuffle between kids, the players gathered for the toss. In my first coin-flip as an international captain, nerves spoiled the occasion. The coin landed down my shirt. When it popped out, it showed heads and I'd lost. As so few players spoke English, I couldn't work out which team was batting and which was bowling. I didn't even know who was in which team.

It appeared my A-team was inserted first. The B medium pacers showed little mercy in their tracksuits, exploiting centre-circle demons to the full. The ball kicked and spat past our openers' heads, and in the follow-up deliveries promptly flattened their stumps. The bails landed in the hands of the old-fashioned backstop.

In a recovery job Kevin Pietersen's mum would have been proud of, our middle order plundered the short, square boundaries. Each four was cheered by players and spectators as though this was a World Cup final. Even the players' girlfriends had turned out to clap and do the scorebook.

At the end of an over I walked down the wicket to discuss tactics with my partner. 'Don't be afraid to pick up your bat and smack it,' I said. My partner stared back, not understanding a word. I realised I'd have to resign my captaincy forthwith. There was no way I'd be able to set fields in the second innings.

After Vladimir's tight mix of pace and spin, the B-team used paper-scissors-stone to decide who'd bowl their final overs. By the end of our allotted twenty, the As had accelerated to 97 for 5. Bearded truck-driver Stalin, one of the four Juricek brothers, had unselfishly guided me to my first international 50. Tired from his 0 not out, he then had to leave to paint his room orange. A substitute was sought from the stands.

At the innings change, a storm began to whip across the field. Entrusted with the new ball by the second captain – a rarity for a leg spinner – I suffered a haunting flashback of my first school match. Back then we played in starched, white school shirts and cream, cotton shorts. We wore knee-high red socks, held up by garters, with combs tucked into their rims.

School rules dictated hair *always* had to be side-parted. As former England managers will testify, this is what made a good cricketer. The wind in that first game caused my hair to fly all over the place. I lost my side parting and my radar. I bowled thirteen wides in a single over. It was a feat that saw me go from the Under-12s' opening paceman to scorer for the rest of the season. As I looked at Lubos facing me now, bent over at a right angle, I had a horrible feeling my international career could meet the same fate.

I approached the wicket and released. Lubos's leg stump was sent cartwheeling backwards. The poor lad had been up since four that morning for work.

Their favoured forward defensive prods à la French cricket couldn't save B's top three being fired out. And when they suffered two direct hit run-outs from the boundary in two balls – the second from a lazily jogged single – it all looked to be over.

But Vladimir, relishing his captain's role, looted the vacant leg-side boundary with sweeps. He gained admirable support from the player selected for university without ever having scored a run. He chose this opportunity to register his personal best. He scored 2, and received the loudest cheer of the day.

In a desperate move, we tried the same bowler from each end in succession. Even this illegal ploy couldn't stop a final stand of 40, and a loss by two wickets, with just one ball to spare.

As Vladimir was carried off the field for his winning 55, thirty villagers cheering, he turned to say, 'This was our greatest ever game!'

David Gower:

In the winter of 1977, I went on a Derrick Robins tour to the Far East and Sri Lanka. One of our first ports of call on the tour was Singapore and as soon as we arrived, one of the senior players (those who were supposed to know what was, and was not, acceptable on tour) volunteered to take the youngsters to Bugis Street.

'What's that then?' we asked naively.

'We'll show you . . .'

And off we went in a rickshaw, visiting a couple of shows en route, where girls did amazing things with ping-pong balls that had not been on the syllabus at King's Canterbury.

Bugis Street doesn't get going until late, so we'd had a few beers by the time we took our seats in a bar populated by what I thought were some strikingly beautiful women. Eventually, of course, the more experienced of my team-mates stopped smirking and let slip that these girls were not quite what they seemed and had bits attached that you would not want to play with.

One person whom I won't name failed to heed all warnings and was taken back to a room by one of these 'ladies', only to end up retreating from it backwards, protecting himself with an outstretched chair rather like a lion-tamer!

Barry Johnston:

By the start of October 2001, Nasser Hussain's lack of success with the coin toss was becoming the stuff of legend. Back in February, long-suffering England cricket fans were already grumbling about the loss of eight tosses out of ten, the odds against which were about 22 to 1. By the end of the summer the England captain had lost twelve tosses in a row, a stunning run with odds against of more than 4000 to 1.

Then on tour in Zimbabwe, Nasser Hussain was injured. Marcus Trescothick took over as the England skipper on 10 October for the fourth One Day International against Zimbabwe, in Bulawayo, and immediately won the toss. Three days later Hussain recovered and returned to the captaincy for the final match in the series – and promptly lost his thirteenth toss in a row!

Marcus Berkmann: Rain Men

The most disastrous excursion ever undertaken by the Captain Scott XI combined the dynamics of a cricket tour (male bonding, alcohol, cheap hotels, desultory sightseeing) with the duration and cost of a real holiday (two weeks, and don't ask). The plan was simple – a week in Hong Kong, a week in Delhi, two games in each.

By the time we returned, thirteen days later, virtually no one was talking to anyone else. Small groupings of people who now loathed each other tactfully avoided saying goodbye while they grabbed their luggage and fled to waiting cabs. At Delhi Airport earlier, at least one punch had been thrown. I myself could barely bring myself to spit the names of at least five returning personnel, while my girlfriend, who had also come on the trip, wanted to murder at least eight. Six days later, she gave me the elbow. I developed amoebic dysentery. Credit-card companies wrote pointed letters. It was quite a trip.

But for a writer, no experience is ever wasted. It is with this in mind that I have devised the Cricket Tour Game, which can be played by anyone venturing abroad for spurious cricketing reasons. Score points as instructed, and add up your total. Depending on your point of view, anyone scoring over 200 has done either very well or very badly indeed.

PART 1: AT THE AIRPORT

You have met at the airport with all your cricketing chums. Score 1 point for any player not there on time. Score 3 points for any player subsequently found hiding in the bar. Score 5 points for every passport that has to be retrieved from a piece of luggage which has already been checked in. Score 10 points for every piece of cricket equipment that goes missing in the process.

PART 2: ON THE AEROPLANE

Long haul, short haul, it doesn't matter. As far as the cricket tourists are concerned, it's time for a drink. Score 4 points for every drink consumed before pubs in England would normally open. Score 5 points for any player who asks for a chaser. Score 1 point for any player who snores loudly during the film. Score 1 point for any player who tries to chat up the stewardess. Score 1 point for each filled barf bag.

PART 3: AT YOUR DESTINATION

Score 2 points for each lost passport, piece of luggage, item of clothing left on plane, etc. Score 5 points for each argument with a passport official. ('Can't you read? I am a British subject.') Score 5 points each time you pass the same landmark in the taxi on the way to the hotel. Score 10 points for each argument with the cab driver. Score 3 points if you have hot water in your room. Score 3 points if you have a window.

PART 4: AT THE MATCH

Score 5 points for each humorous 'local rule' dreamed up by the opposition to hamper your efforts. Score 2 points for every terrible lbw decision. If on the Indian subcontinent, score 10 points for every serious stomach ailment contracted from lunch. Score 1 point for every foreign passerby who stops to look at you as though you are mad. Score 1 point for every 36-shot film of useless 'action photos' you take. Score 5 points for any player who forgets his cap and contracts mild sunstroke.

PART 5: SIGHTSEEING

Score 10 points for every player who claims to be fluent in the local language. Score 200 points for every player who really is fluent in the local language. Score 1 point for each unnecessary item you buy, plus an extra point if you have been gratuitously ripped off for it. Score 15 points for each unnecessary item you later manage to palm off on an unsuspecting friend or relative.

PART 6: LATE-NIGHT ENTERTAINMENT

Score 25 points for any player (without wife or girlfriend present) who says that he fancies an early night tonight, if that's all right by everyone, and he'll see them all at breakfast. Score 5 points for any player who manages to get through the evening without buying a drink. (Score an extra 50 if that player is you, but only if no one notices.) Score 5 points for anyone who pompously pronounces on the intrinsic superiority of the local beer. Score 2 points for any player who decides to try a local liqueur, 2 more if he pretends to like it, 20 points if he actually likes it. Score 1 point for any player telling any other player at three in the morning, 'You know, Cliff, you're a f***ing good bloke, you really are.'

PART 7: BLOW-UP

Score 1 point for every punch thrown. Score 1 point for every swear word. Score 50 points if you manage to keep out of it completely.

PART 8: THE JOURNEY HOME

Score 5 points per argument, plus an extra 5 if it is with the cab driver again and an extra 10 if the police have to be called. Score 1 point for every player drunk before he gets on the plane. Score 5 points for every player 'accidentally' tripped up in the aisle on his way to the loo. Score 2 points for every player who said he definitely ordered the vegetarian meal, even though you know he didn't. Score 1 point for everyone who says we saw this film on the trip out. Score 1 point for each lost passport, piece of luggage, etc. at the airport. Score 50 points if you speak to any of them ever again.

EXTRAS

Mike Selvey:

It is a gloriously sunny day in early June and the crowds are already milling along the St John's Wood Road, chattering animatedly as they make their way towards the Grace Gates. It is Test match day at Lord's. A white Jaguar noses noiselessly past cabs dropping members off, and pulls up at the gates. The occupant, blond, six feet eight inches tall, and pretty recognisable in these parts, waits patiently for the gates to swing open and admit him. He waits in vain until at last they open a crack and an elderly gent walks out and peers myopically into the car. The driver pushes a button and the window hisses down. 'Can I see your pass, sir?' asks the old man.

The only thing that Tony Greig could do was laugh. He might as well have done; everyone else did. 'Sorry, I haven't got one,' he replied.

'Well, you can't come in here, then,' the England captain was told, and the man shambled back inside and closed the gates once more.

If the England captain couldn't get into the

headquarters of cricket, what hope is there for the rest of us? The short answer is none. Once, when I played for Middlesex, I was refused entry to the ground on the morning of a big match, a cup semi-final maybe, by someone with whom I had passed pleasantries on probably half the summers' mornings for the previous ten years.

On another occasion, a policeman actually reached in through my car window during an inquisition at the gate and confiscated my keys to prevent me getting further. And once I was not allowed into the Pavilion 'because Middlesex aren't at home today'. I would not have minded so much if it had been a Test or something, but it was 4 January, the snow lay thick on the ground, and I had only called in while passing to wish people a Happy New Year!

Barry Johnston:

The former Prime Minister Sir John Major had to give up playing cricket in the 1960s after he injured his leg in a very serious car crash in Nigeria. Many years later he was introduced to a woman who claimed to have mystical powers. Recalling the incident in a speech at the National Sporting Club in 1991, John Major said that the woman told him, very apologetically, that his car accident had been a mistake. She explained, 'It should have happened to the car in front.'

Major was not quite sure how to respond to that, so he asked her, 'Well, can fate put my leg back together again?'

'Much too difficult,' said the mystic. 'Leg broken, ligaments torn, kneecap smashed, not a hope of putting it together again. But I can probably give you a wish as a consolation prize.'

'Excellent,' said Major. 'Please spare us an England middle order collapse in the next Test match.'

The mystic paused and said, 'Let me have another look at that leg!'

Henry Blofeld:

Brian Johnston used to ring me up and tell me silly stories. The telephone went one morning and he said, 'Do you know the one about the jump leads?'

I said, 'No.'

Johnners said, 'There was this chap who got an invitation to a fancy-dress ball at the Dorchester Hotel and it said: P.S. Bring the invitation with you. So off he went, but he went naked. He wore nothing but jump leads all over him. He arrived at the hotel entrance and the doorman stopped him, saying, "You can't come in here like that!"

'The man said, "I've come to the party. Here's my invitation."

'"But it's a fancy-dress party," insisted the doorman. "You can't possibly come in looking like that."

'The man said, "But I am *in* fancy dress."

'"What on earth have you come as?"

'He replied, "Why, any fool can see what I've come as . . . I've come as a set of jump leads."

'The doorman rather grudgingly admitted, "Well, yes . . . I suppose you have," and he stood aside to let him go through into the hotel.

'As he went inside, the doorman shouted after him, "But don't you start anything!"'

Simon Hughes:

One day I was twelfth man at Lord's and I was having a breather on the balcony after the morning chores, watching Wilf Slack bat. Suddenly he larruped one straight into the Northants short-leg's head. The fielder sank to the ground in agony and all the Middlesex players looked at me as if it were my fault. 'Go on, hurry up, get the physio – he might be dying,' said the coach.

The Middlesex physiotherapist was Johnny Miller, a frail elderly man, who was almost blind. Miller was in his room and when I burst in, he sensed something was wrong.

'What is it, mate?' he asked. 'An MCC member with convulsions?'

'No, something serious – Geoff Cook's been hit on the head.'

'Quick, lead me out,' he said, panicking, and grabbed his first-aid satchel, knocking bottles off the medicine cabinet in the process.

I helped him downstairs and through the Long Room, but when we were out on the field he let go of my hand and suddenly blundered ahead. He lurched towards a group of players crowded round the stricken Cook, then suddenly veered off course and made straight for the wicketkeeper, George Sharp, who was minding his own business by the stumps.

'Where's the problem, mate?' Miller asked, and started feeling Sharp's face. 'Oh yes, a nasty bump there.'

'That's my gumshield,' said Sharp. 'The injured player's over there!'

Matthew Engel: (from Wisden Cricketers' Almanack 2012)

In 2011, a white tiger stopped play for twenty minutes between Hampshire Academy and South Wiltshire at the Rose Bowl, Southampton. The police had received a call alerting them to the beast's presence in a nearby field. Officers went to the scene and, said a spokesman, 'They confirmed they were looking at it, and it was looking at them.'

The cricketers and golfers on a nearby course were told to go indoors; a helicopter was scrambled; a team from Marwell Zoo was put on standby with tranquilliser darts; and contingency plans were made to close the M27.

It was only when police on the ground noticed the tiger was not moving, and the helicopter team said its thermal imaging cameras could not find a heat source, that officers realised that they were *indeed* confronted with a tiger.

A stuffed toy one.

Ricky Ponting:

We were on a plane to India for the 1996 World Cup, and I was seated in an aisle seat for the first leg of our flight, from Sydney to Bangkok, next to Steve Waugh. Michael Slater was sitting directly across from me, and he noticed me studying the flash Thai Airways International showbag.

'It's just toiletries, mate,' he said helpfully. 'Try the breath freshener.'

I unzipped the bag, went through the soap, toothpaste, breath freshener … no, that's the shaving cream … deodorant. Finally, I found the breath freshener, but initially I was worried it might be an elaborate trap. What was Slats up to? I took the cap off the small bottle, and gave the button a gentle prod, so that just a smidgen of spray came out.

Hey, that's not too bad, I thought to myself, as I nodded in Slats's direction. Then I looked to my right and saw that rather than checking out what freebies might be on offer, Steve Waugh was intently studying the new laptop one of his sponsors had given him to help him type his next best-selling tour diary. He hadn't heard what Slats and I had been talking about.

'Hey, Tugga, have you tried the breath freshener,' I asked, as I passed a bottle over to him.

'Thanks, mate,' he replied, as he put the nozzle to his mouth and pushed hard.

But it wasn't the breath freshener; it was the shaving cream. I'd done him beautifully. He spat the foam out all over his new laptop, muttered something about me being a 'little prick', and then had to call a flight attendant over to clean up the mess!

Once that was done, he looked over at me and said, 'Don't worry, young fella. I've got a memory like an elephant.'

He has, too!

Brian Johnston:

I heard this story from the veteran comedy actor Naunton Wayne, who starred in the Alfred Hitchcock film

The Lady Vanishes, and was a great cricket fan. Before the start of a needle village match, the home captain found he was one short. In desperation he was looking round the ground for someone he could rope in to play when he spotted an old horse grazing quietly in the field next door. So he went up to him and asked him if he would like to make up the side. The horse stopped eating and said, 'Well, I haven't played for some time and am a bit out of practice but if you're pushed, I'll certainly help you out,' and so saying jumped over the fence and sat down in a deck chair in front of the pavilion.

The visitors lost the toss and the home side batted first, the horse being put in last. They were soon 23 for 9 and the horse made his way to the wicket wearing those sort of leather shoes horses have on when they are pulling a roller or a mower. He soon showed his eye was well in and hit the bowling all over the field. When he wasn't hitting sixes he was galloping for quick singles and never once said 'Neigh' when his partner called him for a run. Finally he was out hoof before wicket for a brilliant 68, and the home side had made 99.

When the visitors batted, the home captain put the horse in the deep and he saved many runs by galloping round the boundary and hoofing the ball back to the wicketkeeper. However, the visitors were not losing any wickets and were soon 50 for 0. The home captain had tried all his regular bowlers in vain when he suddenly thought of the horse. He had batted brilliantly and now was fielding better than anyone. At least he could do no worse than the other bowlers. So he called out to him, 'Horse, would you like to take the next over at the vicarage end?'

The horse looked surprised, 'Of course I wouldn't,' he replied. 'Whoever heard of a horse who could *bowl*!'

Alastair Cook:

My mind was made up during the Third Test against India at Trent Bridge in 2018. I texted my wife Alice, 'Are you OK? I've got to tell you this. The end of this series is going to be my last game for England.' I told Jimmy Anderson first, as we sat on the balcony watching the day's play, then Rooty and Broady, and finally the England coach, Trevor Bayliss. I knew my secret was safe with them.

Immediately after we clinched the series by winning that Test, Trevor and Rooty led a happy dressing-room debrief, before handing over to me. I was a few beers in at that time, to quell the nerves, because I didn't know how I was going to react to telling the rest of the lads. I didn't go full Oscar acceptance speech, but my voice caught a couple of times.

'This might be a sad day for some people or a happy day for others,' I announced, 'but I just want to let you know that my next Test, if picked, will be my last. I've run out of steam and this has been a great way to finish.'

Sportsmen take the piss at every opportunity, of course, so I didn't get away scot free. I had wanted to come across as thoughtful, despite the intensity of emotion I felt, so ended with a light-hearted apology for dampening the mood.

Moeen Ali, who has a dry sense of humour and a quick wit, shot back.

'Well, you just have, haven't you!'

Not his best line perhaps, but enough to crack everyone up.

Michael Simkins: Fatty Batter

One of the wonderful things about cricket is the way it throws up unlikely heroes. The Harry Baldwin Occasionals

XI away against Worthing Railways is just such an occasion.

The venue is Patcham Place and the match is supposed to begin at 2 p.m., but by 3.15 it has yet to commence. Of the eleven players who should have turned up for the Baldwins, so far we have four. A glance at the main road skirting the ground is all that's needed to see what the problem is. Patcham Place runs directly alongside the main A23 London to Brighton road, and today's match has coincided with the annual London to Brighton cycle rally, in aid of the British Heart Foundation. There are between 25,000 and 30,000 cyclists all approaching the town centre along a twenty-mile stretch of the A23, behind which founders a vehicle traffic jam that is already stretching back nearly fifteen miles. Somewhere in the middle of that lot, cooking quietly on a low heat, is the cream of today's Baldwin team.

Which leaves myself, Keith the Cub Scout leader, whom I rang twenty minutes ago to whisk away from his youngest's birthday party, and finally our impromptu substitute, Gordon Quill.

Quill is one of the curios of the side. He readily admits to being hopeless at the game but likes to come along to watch and afterwards enjoy a blackcurrant and lemonade in the pub with us all. He doesn't really play much, but deals in antique Victoriana, and he's only come along to today's match in order to show me his collection of antique seaside postcards he picked up at an auction in Lewes last week.

The Worthing Railways captain comes up to me. A large bluff man called Frank, he works as a ticket inspector on the Three Bridges to Arundel spur.

'How many are you now?'

'Um . . .'

'Never mind. Let's go.'

'Of course, of course. It's just that . . .'

'What?'

'Well, it's just that we forgot it was the bike rally today . . .'

'Tough.' In his professional life Frank is used to lame excuses and pleas of ignorance. 'We'll lend you a couple of fielders till they arrive.'

He pulls on his batting gloves and summons his opening partner to join him in the middle. I call across to Quill who is just showing a first-edition postcard of Donald McGill's 'I Can't Find My Little Willy' to the Worthing Railways wicketkeeper.

'Gordon, you're going to have to open the bowling.'

Having Gordon Quill open the bowling is a bit like asking my mum to front a twelve-part television cookery course. But the fact is there's nobody else. At least Quill can just about propel it down the other end. We'll get through his first over and then regroup. Perhaps somebody else might have turned up by then.

The Railwaymen have lent us three of their team, all of whom are standing sulkily in the outfield waiting to be positioned. I hand Quill the match ball provided by the opposition, a gleaming rock-hard cherry still in its tissue paper, and retire to mid-off to consider my tactical options.

There's no delaying the inevitable. Quill approaches off a run-up of about three inches, and whirls his arm over. The ball bounces three times before coming to rest just in front of Frank's motionless figure at the crease. Frank removes his helmet and stares over at me with a look of withering disdain.

'Is he taking the piss?'

'Not at all.'

'This is your opening bowler, is it?'

I scan the roadside before replying. Just an endless crawl of slowly moving traffic. 'Just at the moment,' I reply.

'Right,' mutters Frank, simply. He picks up the ball and throws it back to Quill. 'Here you are, Dr Livingstone,' he says. Quill marches back to his run-up and sets off again.

Three seconds later, via a brief but violent interruption in its trajectory from Frank's bat, the ball soars over my head at extra cover, hits a tree on the boundary half-way up its trunk, ricochets into the road where it nearly decapitates a member of the Crawley Down Road Racing

319

team, before bouncing off the far pavement and coming to rest against the wall of the Black Lion Hotel. Keith trots off to fetch it, but with the cyclists still surging past in an endless flood, the simple act of crossing and re-crossing the road eats up a further five minutes.

The next ball is hit with such force that it breaks a security light outside the front door of the YMCA hostel at the far end of the ground. Quill looks nervously over at me, but I give him a thumbs-up sign to indicate he's doing just fine. Frank thrashes his next delivery as hard as he can straight back at the bowler, but fortunately it narrowly misses Quill and cannons into the far set of stumps beside him, not only preventing any runs from being scored but breaking one of the bails in the process. Further minutes tick by while some binding tape is found from the pavilion and the wicket is repaired.

Quill's fifth delivery is flayed over extra cover, where it strikes the hub cap of a Peugeot 406 travelling on the main road, and rebounds back on to the field of play. My heart momentarily leaps: perhaps the driver will pull over, using up yet more time. But he drives on, oblivious. Funny how when luck's against you . . .

But at last fortune turns my way. Quill's last delivery is smashed for six high over the mid-wicket boundary, where it lands deep into a huge bank of nettles and fallen tree trunks brought down by the great storm of 1985.

After furious exhortations from Frank to the pavilion, his grumbling colleagues eventually rise from their deck-chairs and begin a slow and painstaking search for the missing ball. Quill turns to me ruefully. 'Sorry old chap,' he says.

But there's no need for an apology. He's playing a blinder. Success on the field is all about percentage cricket, and with the current wage restraint being imposed on British Rail platform staff combined with a brand new cricket ball retailing at nearly fifteen quid a pop, there's no way this lot are going to give up the hunt for it easily. By the time the precious ball is found lying behind a rotting tree stump, the clock on the YMCA building is showing nearly 4 o'clock.

The Railwaymen celebrate the discovery with a yell of triumph, but even as the ball is being thrown back on to the pitch, I spot our first-change bowler Rex Scudamore's Volvo pulling into the car park at the far end. What's more he's already changed into his whites and is ready to play. Phil Coleridge's Renault is only thirty yards behind. I celebrate by giving my emergency bowler a huge hug of gratitude. The hits into the cyclists, the broken bail, and the disappearance among the nettles: Quill's single over may have conceded thirty runs, but crucially it has occupied nearly half an hour. He's got us through our crisis. Mafeking has been relieved. Game on.

MATCH REPORT:

Harry Baldwins vs Worthing Railways
Worthing Railways 103 all out off 18 overs
(Quill 0–30, Scudamore 5–22)
Baldwins 104–4
Harry Baldwins win by 6 wickets

Barry Johnston:

It was the first day of a recent Ashes Test at Lord's. A smartly dressed, athletic figure strode up to the Grace Gates to collect his ticket, which had been left for him by one of the England players. He approached one of the famous Lord's gatemen.

'Excuse me, has a ticket for Lord Coe been left here by one of the players?'

'I'll have a look, sir, but I don't remember any name like that. No . . . I am afraid there isn't.'

'Are you sure? It's for Lord Coe, Chairman of the British Olympic Association and the President of World Athletics.'

'No, I'm sorry, sir. But sometimes tickets are left at the North Gate on the other side of the ground.'

'No, he definitely said the Grace Gates. Surely you recognise me? I'm Sebastian Coe, the double Olympic gold medallist and world record breaker in the 800 metres, 1500 metres and the mile.'

'Well, I wouldn't know about that, sir, but if you really are Sebastian Coe, it shouldn't take you too long to run round to the North Gate!'

'AGGERS, DO STOP IT!'

Barry Johnston:

Before the start of the regular *Test Match Special* broadcast in the summer of 1993 there was an extra half-hour programme at 10.30 a.m. on Radio Five, presented by Jonathan Agnew. It began with an upbeat signature tune which required Jonathan to give a summary of the state of play in exactly seven seconds, sounding more like a Radio One disc-jockey than a Radio Three cricket commentator. He used to practise it over and over in order to get the timing right and Brian Johnston always found it most amusing.

On the Sunday morning of the Test match at Headingley, Brian was the first one in the commentary box as usual, when Peter Baxter, the *Test Match Special* producer, rushed in to say that Agnew was going to be late and he would have to do the Radio Five programme instead. With only minutes to spare, Brian had to write and rehearse his seven-second summary, speaking ever faster over the signature tune, as Baxter kept urging him to do it one more time. 'Still a bit long, Johnners . . .

need to lose another second if you can . . .' After several, increasingly frantic, attempts it was time to go on air and, being the consummate professional, Brian did it perfectly.

It was only then that Agnew burst laughing into the box and Brian realised that he had been had. There *was* no Radio Five programme on Sunday morning. The engineers had recorded the whole episode and for the rest of the day Agnew gleefully played the tape to anyone who would listen, saying that Brian had been unable to get the summary right. 'In fact he was spot on first time,' recalls Baxter, 'as I knew he would be.'

'It made up into a brilliant tape,' says Richie Benaud. 'It was funny and a very good practical joke which Brian took in good part. Trouble was, Aggers wanted to tell the world about it. I thought at the time that this could be a very dangerous thing to do.'

Brian did not wait long to exact his revenge. 'He worked on the basis of never get angry, just get even,' adds Benaud, 'and when he played a joke it was always a beauty. The one he came up with during the next Test at Edgbaston was a ripper. It remains my favourite.'

On the Saturday morning of the match Keith Mackenzie, the producer/director of BBC TV cricket, approached Agnew and asked him if he would record an interview for *Grandstand* during the lunch interval. The subject was to be England's lack of fast bowlers. The interview had to be precisely ten minutes long and hard-hitting in content. Mackenzie also dropped a hint that there might at some stage be a place for someone new in the television team.

Agnew readily agreed and that lunchtime he sat in front of the cameras with Fred Trueman and Jack Bannister, both former fast bowlers and now respected cricket experts, to record the interview. Trueman was puffing on a huge cigar which he blew over Agnew just before they began. Undeterred, Agnew put his first question to Bannister, who replied bluntly, 'I've got no idea.' He turned quickly to Trueman, who took another long puff on his cigar and muttered darkly, 'Don't know.'

Agnew began to sweat, not helped by Keith Mackenzie yelling in his earpiece that it was the worst interview he had ever seen. The minutes ticked slowly by. Trueman, when asked about pitches, wandered off into a dissertation on fly-fishing and its benefits to fast bowlers in the strengthening of the shoulder muscles. Bannister contributed an unrelated story about the wrist spinner Eric Hollies and how he almost won a game against Lindsay Hassett's Australian side in 1953. The final straw was when Trueman began talking about damp-proof courses.

At the end of the longest ten minutes in his life, Agnew handed back to the mythical *Grandstand* studio in despair, saying, 'I don't think we have answered too many questions there, gentlemen.' He sat stunned in his chair, imagining his television career to be in ruins. Suddenly his earpiece crackled into life. 'I think the veteran long-nosed commentator might have got his revenge!' chuckled a well-known voice. Brian had been sitting alongside Keith Mackenzie throughout the interview.

He had persuaded the whole of the BBC TV outside broadcast team to give up their lunch break, simply to set up Agnew. You did not beat the Master that easily!

Brian Johnston:

I've said that cricket is fun. Now I want you to cast your mind back to August 1991, the Friday of The Oval Test match against the West Indies. Bad light stopped play at half past six and Peter Baxter, our producer, turned to Jonathan Agnew and myself and said, 'Go through the scorecard, will you please, to fill in time.'

Gallantly, I started the scorecard. I got down as far as Ian Botham, who had been out 'hit wicket' and this is what followed:

Johnners: Botham, in the end, out in the most extraordinary way.
Aggers: Oh, it was ever so sad really. It was interesting, because we were talking and he had just started to

loosen up. He had started to look, perhaps, for the big blows through the off side, for anything a little bit wide – and I remember saying, 'It looks as if Ian Botham is just starting to play his old way.'

It was a bouncer and he tried to hook it. Why he tried to hook Ambrose, I'm not sure, because on this sort of pitch it's a very difficult prospect. It smacked him on the helmet, I think – I'm not quite sure where it did actually hit him . . .

Johnners: Shoulder, I think.

Aggers: Shoulder, was it? As he tried to hook, he lost his balance, and he knew – this is the tragic thing about it – he knew exactly what was going to happen. He tried to step over the stumps and just flicked a bail with his right pad.

Johnners: He more or less tried to do the splits over it and, unfortunately, the inner part of his thigh must have just removed the bail.

Aggers: He just didn't quite get his leg over!

Johnners: Anyhow (*chuckles*) . . . (*clatter as Bill Frindall drops his stopwatch in surprise*) . . . he did very well indeed, batting one hundred and thirty-one minutes and hit three fours . . . (*Agnew buries his face in his hands and starts to giggle helplessly*) . . . and then we had Lewis playing extremely well for forty-seven not out . . . Aggers, do stop it . . . (*Frindall laughs in background*) . . . and he was joined by DeFreitas who was in for forty minutes, a useful little partnership there. They put on thirty-five in forty minutes and then he was caught by Dujon off Walsh . . . (*snort from Frindall*). Lawrence, always entertaining, batted for thirty-five . . . (*Johnners starts to wheeze*) . . . thirty-five . . . (*gasping*) . . . minutes . . . hit a four over the wicket-keeper's h . . . (*high-pitched giggle*) . . . Aggers, for goodness sake stop it! . . . he hit a f . . . (*dissolves into uncontrollable laughter. Peter Baxter hisses at Agnew to say something.*)

Aggers: Yes, Lawrence . . . extremely well . . . (*collapses completely*).

Both men are now speechless with laughter, tears rolling down their faces. Agnew turns desperately for help to Tony Cozier, sitting at the microphone on his left, busily writing an article on his word-processor. Cozier – a frequent victim of Brian's practical jokes – looks up and winks at Agnew, grins and carries on with his typing. Brian tries gamely to continue with the scorecard.

Johnners: (*Hysterical*) . . . He hit . . . (*his voice getting higher and higher*) he hit a four over the wicketkeeper's head and he was out for nine . . . (*crying and dabbing at his eyes with a large handkerchief*) . . . and Tufnell came in and batted for twelve minutes, then he was caught by Haynes off Patterson for two . . .

(*calming down gradually*) . . . and there were fifty-four extras and England were all out for four hundred and nineteen . . . I've stopped laughing now . . .

Barry Johnston:

Next morning the letters and phone calls started to flood in to the *Test Match Special* commentary box. Thousands of drivers had been listening in their cars on their way home and many of them had been forced to pull into the side of the road until they had calmed down. Tim Rice laughed so hard that he thought he was going to endanger his fellow motorists. Ronnie Corbett rang to say that his wife Ann had to stop on the hard shoulder of the M1.

A listener called Paul Brookbanks wrote that he was laughing out loud when he pulled up behind a police car at some roadworks in Peterborough. The policeman got out of his car and walked slowly back to the driver to ask him exactly what he found so amusing – just as Brian returned to normal. The poor man tried to explain that he had been listening to a cricket commentary on the radio, but he could tell that the policeman did not believe a word of it.

Another listener, Jane Wardman from Leeds, had been confined to bed for several weeks with pneumonia. She was feeling fed-up and depressed. Then she heard the 'leg-over' incident on the radio and for the first time in many weeks, wrote Jane, 'laughed until the tears streamed down my face'.

There were even reports of a two-mile tail-back at the entrance to the Dartford Tunnel on the M25, because some drivers were laughing so much that they were unable to go through the toll-booths.

On the Monday following the broadcast the BBC's Head of Litigation, Diana Adie, received an urgent fax from Tony Alexander, a solicitor with a firm called Heffrons in Milton Keynes. It read as follows:

Dear Sir,

Re: Cricket Commentary – Friday 9 August 1991.

We have been consulted by Mr Wally Painter and his wife Dolly. On Friday evening our clients were in the process of redecorating their hallway. Mr Painter was perched on a ladder in the stairwell of his house, whilst Mrs Painter held the ladder steady. Our clients' aquarium with assorted tropical fish was situated at the foot of the stairwell.

Our clients are keen cricket enthusiasts, and were listening to the summary of the day's play on Radio Three, when Mr Brian Johnston and Mr Jon Agnew were discussing Mr Ian Botham's dismissal, which apparently involved some footwork which Mr Botham failed to consummate.

The ensuing events caused a vibration in the ladder and, in spite of Mrs Painter's firm grasp, Mr Painter fell off the ladder, landing awkwardly on the partial landing, thereby dislocating his left wrist. The ladder fell on Mrs Painter, who suffered a contusion to her forehead.

The 5 litre drum of Dulux Sandalwood Emulsion fell and crashed through the aquarium, which flooded the hallway, depositing various frantically flapping exotic fish onto a Persian rug. The Painters' pedigree

Persian cat (Mr Painter spent many years in Tehran as an adviser to the late Shah) grabbed one of the fish, a Malayan red-spined Gurnot, and promptly choked to death.

The water seeped down into the cellar where the electricity meters are located. There were several short circuits, which resulted in (a) the main switchboard being severely damaged and (b) the burglar alarm (which is connected to the local police station) being set off.

Meanwhile, Mr and Mrs Painter were staggering towards the bathroom, apparently in paroxysms of hysterical laughter despite their injuries. Within minutes, the police arrived, and believing the Painters to be vandals and suspecting, as both were incoherent, that they had been taking drugs, promptly arrested them.

We are now instructed to inform you that our clients hold the Corporation liable for:-

(a) Their personal injuries.
(b) The loss of the aquarium and various exotic fish collected over several years.
(c) The damage to the Persian rug.
(d) Damage to the electrical installation and burglar alarm.
(e) Death of the cat.

However, they are prepared to settle all claims for damages in respect of the above provided that you supply them with a recording of the discussion between Mr Johnston and Mr Agnew, together with an undertaking from Mr Johnston and Mr Agnew that they will not in future discuss Mr Botham's foot-work or lack of it, while Mr and Mrs Painter are decorating their property.

Yours faithfully,
Heffrons.

I am happy to report that the Painters received their tape.

ACKNOWLEDGEMENTS

I would like to express my grateful thanks to all the authors and publishers who have given their permission for extracts from their work to be reproduced in this book.

Special thanks go to my father Brian Johnston, Dickie Bird and Henry Blofeld for their hilarious stories on the bestselling *The Wit of Cricket* CD, which got the ball rolling back in 2004. Without them, the first edition of this book would never have happened.

I would also like to thank Tony Alexander for the use of his letter about the Ian Botham 'leg-over' incident. My special thanks to John Ireland as always for his brilliant illustrations. I am also most grateful to Rupert Lancaster and Roddy Bloomfield at Hodder & Stoughton for their invaluable advice, and to Rupert in particular for his continuing support over the past twenty years. Thanks also to Ciara Mongey and the team at Hodder and to Marion Paull for her excellent work in copyediting the original manuscript and to Simon Fox for his meticulous proofreading of the second edition.

For this new, updated edition, I would like to give many thanks to Jonathan Agnew, Peter Baxter and Daniel Norcross for their additional humorous tales from the *Test Match Special* commentary box, and my grateful thanks to Judy Martin-Jenkins for allowing me to include some of the lovely anecdotes by her late husband, Christopher Martin-Jenkins.

Extracts from the following books and audiobooks have been reproduced by kind permission of their publishers or their authors:

Agnew, Jonathan, *Thanks, Johnners* (Blue Door, 2010)
Anderson, Jimmy, *Bowl. Sleep. Repeat.* (Cassell, 2019)
Atherton, Michael, *Opening Up* (Hodder & Stoughton, 2003)

Bairstow, Jonny, *A Clear Blue Sky* (HarperCollins, 2017)

Bell, Angus, *Batting on the Bosphorus: A Škoda-powered cricket tour through Eastern Europe* (Canongate Books, 2008)

Benaud, Richie, *My Spin on Cricket* (Hodder & Stoughton, 2005)

Berkmann, Marcus, *Rain Men* (Little, Brown Book Group, 1995)

Bird, Dickie, *White Cap and Bails* (Hodder & Stoughton, 1999)

Blofeld, Henry, *Cricket's Great Entertainers* (Hodder & Stoughton, 2003)

Brayshaw, Ian, *The Wit of Cricket* (The Currawong Press, Sydney, 1981)

Connelly, Charlie (ed.), *Elk Stopped Play* (Wisden, an imprint of Bloomsbury, 2014)

Cook, Alastair, *The Autobiography* (Michael Joseph, 2019)

Engel, Matthew (ed.), *What Did You Say Stopped Play?* (Bloomsbury, 2018, from *Wisden Cricketers' Almanack*, 1998, 2012, 2016, © John Wisden & Co Ltd)

England, Chris, *Balham to Bollywood* (Hodder & Stoughton, 2002)

Flintoff, Andrew, *Being Freddie* (Hodder & Stoughton, 2005)

Fowler, Graeme, *Fox on the Run* (Viking, 1988)

Frindall, Bill, *Bearders: My Life in Cricket* (Orion, 2006)

Gough, Darren, *Dazzler: The Autobiography* (Michael Joseph, 2001)

Gower, David, *An Endangered Species* (Simon & Schuster, 2013)

Hayden, Matthew, *Standing My Ground* (Penguin Group, Australia, 2010)

Heald, Tim (ed.), *My Lord's* (CollinsWillow, 1990)

Holding, Michael, *No Holding Back* (Weidenfeld & Nicolson, 2010)

Hughes, Simon, *A Lot of Hard Yakka* (Headline, 1997)

Johnson, Martin, *Can't Bat, Can't Bowl, Can't Field* (CollinsWillow, 1997)

Johnston, Barry, *Johnners: The Life of Brian* (Hodder & Stoughton, 2003)

Johnston, Brian & Johnston, Barry, *An Evening with Johnners* (Partridge Press, 1996)

Johnston, Brian, *The Wit of Cricket* (Leslie Frewin, 1968)

Jupp, Miles, *Fibber in the Heat* (Ebury Press, 2012)

Langer, Justin, *Keeping My Head* (Allen & Unwin, Australia, 2010)

Lloyd, David, *The Autobiography* (CollinsWillow, 2000)

Marks, Vic, *Original Spin* (Allen & Unwin, 2019)

Morgan-Grenville, Roger, *Unlimited Overs* (Quiller, 2019)

Parkinson, Michael, *On Cricket* (Hodder & Stoughton, 2003)

Pietersen, Kevin, *Crossing the Boundary* (Ebury, 2006)

Ponting, Ricky, *At the Close of Play* (HarperCollins, Australia, UK, and India, 2013)

Rice, Jonathan (ed.), *Classic After-Dinner Sports Tales* (CollinsWillow, 2004)

Root, Joe, *Bringing Home the Ashes* (Hodder & Stoughton, 2015)

Simkins, Michael, *Fatty Batter* (Ebury, 2007)

Stokes, Ben, *Firestarter* (Headline, 2016)

Stokes, Ben, *On Fire* (Headline, 2019)

Strauss, Andrew, *Coming into Play* (Hodder & Stoughton, 2006)

Tendulkar, Sachin, *Playing It My Way* (Hodder & Stoughton, 2014)

Thompson, Harry, *Penguins Stopped Play* (John Murray, 2006)

Trueman, Fred, *As It Was* (Pan Macmillan, 2004)

Trueman, Fred & Mosey, Don, *Talking Cricket* (Hodder & Stoughton, 1997)

Vaughan, Michael, *A Year in the Sun* (Hodder & Stoughton, 2003)

Warne, Shane, *My Autobiography* (Hodder & Stoughton, 2001)

AUDIOBOOKS:

Baxter, Peter; Johnston, Barry; Martin-Jenkins, Christopher; Powell, Robert, *The Wit of Cricket at Home and Abroad* (Hodder & Stoughton Audiobooks, 2010)

Bird, Dickie, *An Evening with Dickie Bird* (Hodder Headline Audiobooks, 1998)

Bird, Dickie; Blofeld, Henry; Johnston, Brian, *The Wit of Cricket* (Hodder Headline Audiobooks, 2004)

Benaud, Richie; Bird, Dickie; Blofeld, Henry; Johnston, Brian; Trueman, Fred, *The Wit of Cricket 2* (Hodder & Stoughton Audiobooks, 2007)

Blofeld, Henry, *An Evening with Blowers* (Hodder Headline Audiobooks, 2002)

Johnston, Brian, *An Evening with Johnners* (Hodder Headline Audiobooks, 2000)

Amongst other books and websites consulted, particular use was made of: Christopher Martin-Jenkins: *The Complete Who's Who of Test Cricketers*; *Wisden Cricketers' Almanack*; *Daily Mail*; bbc.co.uk; espncricinfo.com; anecdotage.com; heraldsun.com.au; indiancricketfans.com. Whilst every effort has been made to trace all copyright holders, the publishers would be pleased to hear from any not here acknowledged.

INDEX